Diseases and Disorders

Bipolar Disorder

Titles in the Diseases and Disorders series include:

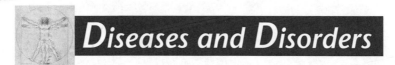

Diseases and Disorders

Bipolar Disorder

by Melissa Abramovitz

LUCENT BOOKS
An imprint of Thomson Gale, a part of The Thomson Corporation

THOMSON
GALE

Detroit • New York • San Francisco • San Diego • New Haven, Conn.
Waterville, Maine • London • Munich

For more information, contact
Lucent Books
27500 Drake Rd.
Farmington Hills, MI 48331-3535
Or you can visit our Internet site at http://www.gale.com

LIBRARY OF CONGRESS CATALOGING-IN-PUBLICATION DATA

Abramovitz, Melissa, 1954–
    Bipolar disorder / by Melissa Abramovitz.
        p. cm. — (Diseases and disorders)
    Includes bibliographical references and index.
    ISBN 1-59018-589-7 (hard cover : alk. paper)
    1. Manic-depressive illness—Juvenile literature. I. Title. II. Series: Diseases and disorders series
    RC516.A27 2004
    616.89'5—dc22

                                                                    2004013919

Printed in the United States of America

Table of Contents

"The Most Difficult Puzzles Ever Devised"

CHARLES BEST, ONE of the pioneers in the search for a cure for diabetes, once explained what it is about medical research that intrigued him so. "It's not just the gratification of knowing one is helping people," he confided, "although that probably is a more heroic and selfless motivation. Those feelings may enter in, but truly, what I find best is the feeling of going toe to toe with nature, of trying to solve the most difficult puzzles ever devised. The answers are there somewhere, those keys that will solve the puzzle and make the patient well. But how will those keys be found?"

Since the dawn of civilization, nothing has so puzzled people—and often frightened them, as well—as the onset of illness in a body or mind that had seemed healthy before. A seizure, the inability of a heart to pump, the sudden deterioration of muscle tone in a small child—being unable to reverse such conditions or even to understand why they occur was unspeakably frustrating to healers. Even before there were names for such conditions, even before they were understood at all, each was a reminder of how complex the human body was, and how vulnerable.

While our grappling with understanding diseases has been frustrating at times, it has also provided some of humankind's most heroic accomplishments. Alexander Fleming's accidental discovery in 1928 of a mold that could be turned into penicillin has resulted in the saving of untold millions of lives. The isolation of the enzyme insulin has reversed what was once a death sentence for anyone with diabetes. There have been great strides in combating conditions for which there is not yet a cure, too. Medicines can help AIDS patients live longer, diagnostic tools such as mammography and ultrasounds can help doctors find tumors while they are treatable, and laser surgery techniques have made the most intricate, minute operations routine.

This "toe-to-toe" competition with diseases and disorders is even more remarkable when seen in a historical continuum. An astonishing amount of progress has been made in a very short time. Just 200 years ago, the existence of germs as a cause of some diseases was unknown. In fact, it was less than 150 years ago that a British surgeon named Joseph Lister had difficulty persuading his fellow doctors that washing their hands before delivering a baby might increase the chances of a healthy delivery (especially if they had just attended to a diseased patient)!

Each book in Lucent's Diseases and Disorders series explores a disease or disorder and the knowledge that has been accumulated (or discarded) by doctors through the years. Each book also examines the tools used for pinpointing a diagnosis, as well as the various means that are used to treat or cure a disease. Finally, new ideas are presented—techniques or medicines that may be on the horizon.

Frustration and disappointment are still part of medicine, for not every disease or condition can be cured or prevented. But the limitations of knowledge are being pushed outward constantly; the "most difficult puzzles ever devised" are finding challengers every day.

An Increasingly Common Disorder

EXPERTS ARE NOT sure how long bipolar disorder, also known as manic-depressive illness, has existed, because there is no evidence of it in ancient records. The illness is characterized by episodes of both depression and mania. Depression, a condition in which a person becomes extremely despondent, was clearly described in Mesopotamian tablets that date as far back as about 2000 B.C., but medical historians are not sure if mania, a state in which someone is frantically full of energy and activity, was identified in these ancient writings. These medical historians do point out that mania and depression in the same person were not linked in ancient records.

The First References to Mania and Depression in the Same Person

It was not until the seventeenth century that doctors began writing about mania and depression in the same patient. Richard Napier, a doctor in England during this time, wrote detailed descriptions of patients whose psychiatric symptoms indicated the high and low mood states that characterize bipolar disorder. In the eighteenth century, more and more cases were documented. Two well-known eighteenth-century authors who suffered from manic depression were Charles Lamb and his sister, Mary Lamb. Mary killed their invalid mother with a carving knife during a violent manic episode; although some bipolar patients can become violent, most do not commit such acts. Mary Lamb's episodes of mania alternated with periods of intense depression for the rest of her life. Mary and Charles Lamb cowrote the children's book *Tales Founded on the Plays of Shakespeare* in spite of the illness they suffered.

By the early nineteenth century, doctors were familiar with manic-depressive illness through its inclusion in medical textbooks such as Philippe Pinel's *Treatise on Insanity* (1806) and John Haslam's *Observations on Madness and Melancholy* (1809). Haslam, for example, described people with mania and depression, saying that those with

Though both had bipolar disorder, eighteenth-century authors Charles Lamb (pictured) and his sister Mary cowrote a famous children's book.

mania "get but little sleep . . . are loquacious [wordy], and disposed to harangue [scold], and decide positively upon every subject that may be started." Those with depression, or melancholia, "wear an anxious and gloomy aspect . . . are little disposed to speak . . . lie in bed the greatest part of the time . . . and endeavor by their own hands to terminate an existence which appears to be an afflicting and hateful incumbrance."[1] Haslam pointed out that many times the same patient would switch from manic to depressive symptoms.

By the end of the nineteenth century, the disease that many doctors came to know as mania alternating with melancholia was named manic-depressive insanity by German psychiatrist Emil Kraepelin. Psychiatrists referred to the disease as manic-depressive illness until 1980, when the American Psychiatric Association changed the name to bipolar disorder. Both terms are used today.

An Increase in Bipolar Cases

Kraepelin and others in his era also noted that the number of people with this illness and other forms of insanity was increasing at an even faster rate than the population of the world. Indeed, in the United States alone, the number of hospitalized insane people more than doubled between 1890 and 1910 and continued to grow in subsequent years. By 1940 the number had tripled from the rate in 1890. Once scientists developed effective medications to treat many mental illnesses in the 1960s, some of these hospitalized patients could be released even though they were not cured. Experts say, however, that the incidence of serious mental illnesses such as manic depression continued to rise even though fewer patients were being hospitalized. One study found that people born after 1935 are more likely to develop bipolar disorder than those born before 1935. No one is sure why this is true; the increase in reported cases could be partly due to better diagnosis of the disease.

As the number of people affected with bipolar disorder rises, the cost in suffering and dollars also rises. According to E. Fuller Torrey and Michael B. Knable,

> The greatest cost of manic-depressive illness is the personal toll it takes on affected individuals and their families. It is also

incalculable. . . . How do you calculate the cost of repairing the consequences when a family member with mania depletes the family's savings account, purchases three cars, and publicly announces he is going to marry a prostitute? How do you calculate the cost of what happens to young children when their mother experiences prolonged, severe, untreated episodes of depression, or the cost of a suicide?[2]

The dollar amount related to bipolar disorder is also high and continues to rise each year as medical costs soar. In addition to the billions of dollars spent on hospitalization, medications, doctor visits, and related costs, there are also billions in indirect costs, such as lost wages when patients cannot work or when family members must take time off to care for them. Federal and state governments also spend billions of dollars in disability and supplemental security payments to patients, so the illness is a financial burden to taxpayers as well.

A concerned therapist counsels a patient with bipolar disorder. Many patients manage the disorder through a combination of therapy and medication.

Experts say that many of these expenses could be reduced if bipolar patients, who often do not think they need medication, would consistently take their medicine to keep the illness under control. Mental health agencies and private doctors are making efforts to educate people on the importance of sticking to a treatment plan, but even those patients who recover with treatment still have the disease. As such, there is a great deal of research underway as scientists try to figure out what causes bipolar disorder in hopes of developing more effective treatments or even a cure for the disease.

Chapter 1

What Is Bipolar Disorder?

BIPOLAR DISORDER IS a brain disorder that causes dramatic shifts in a person's mood, energy level, and ability to function. These shifts are much more severe than the normal ups and downs that most people experience, and the moods do not go away on their own and cannot be shaken off. Bipolar disorder is a disease, just like heart disease or diabetes, except that it affects the brain. It is generally a chronic, or long-term, disease. Once someone has it, it does not usually go away, at least not permanently. About 25 percent of people with the disease recover with treatment, 10 to 20 percent have severe, ongoing mood-swing episodes, and 55 to 65 percent partially recover and can lead reasonably normal lives.

Because it mainly affects mood, bipolar disorder is known as a mood, or affective, disorder. The illness affects more than just mood, however. It also impacts thoughts and behaviors to the extent that the patient's life is totally disrupted. The individual goes from overly "high" and energetic to sad and hopeless, then back again. These mood swings can last for hours, days, weeks, or months, depending on the particular patient. In between these extreme episodes of highs and lows, or mania and depression, can be periods of normal mood and energy, although some people never experience relief from these states. The name *bipolar disorder* or *manic-depressive illness* refers to the fact that affected persons go from one extreme polarity of mania to one of depression.

Typical Symptoms of Mania

Bipolar patients can have some or all of the typical symptoms of mania or depression. One of the primary symptoms of mania is increased

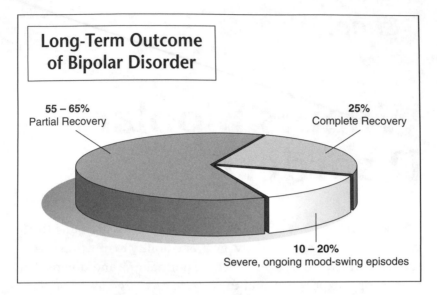

Long-Term Outcome of Bipolar Disorder

55 – 65%
Partial Recovery

25%
Complete Recovery

10 – 20%
Severe, ongoing mood-swing episodes

energy, activity, and restlessness, where the person never stops doing things or starting new projects. This frantic activity often goes along with a lack of tiredness and little need for sleep. Some patients do not sleep for days at a time, and some have pushed themselves to exhaustion and even death with nonstop activity. One patient succumbed to exhaustion after not sleeping for about two weeks.

Some patients with mania experience an excessively euphoric mood, feeling as though anything is possible and everything is great. Along with this euphoria often goes a disregard for risk that leads to risk-taking behavior, as these individuals believe nothing bad will happen. Rose, a child with bipolar disorder, for instance, tried to jump out of a moving car.

Other patients show extreme irritability and aggression, and their hyperactivity centers on hostility and dissatisfaction with everything around them. This pattern of symptoms is especially prevalent in children with bipolar disorder. Nine-year-old Jerry, for example, suffered from extreme irritability and would throw tantrums and tear apart his room during manic episodes.

Racing thoughts, or jumping from one idea to another, is also common during mania. As one patient describes it, "Thoughts whiz through your brain like enormous meteor showers."[3] In addition to having racing thoughts, the person talks very fast or changes topics rapidly. People who are manic cannot seem to stop talking or switching from one idea to another. They often interrupt others and take over conversations. And they cannot concentrate well on a single task, because they keep switching gears so rapidly.

An unrealistic belief in one's abilities and power is another hallmark of a manic state. Jennie believed she was going to save the world. Others in the throes of mania may believe they are famous actors or writers, or they have other delusions (unrealistic beliefs that are not true). Others believe they can heal people by touching them or that they can read other people's thoughts.

Along with these unrealistic beliefs may go poor judgment, as when patients with bipolar disorder suddenly quit their jobs because they believe they are independently wealthy. Spending sprees due to delusions of wealth are also common. Jennie, a teen with bipolar disorder, bought one thousand dollars worth of clothes

Like this adolescent, some young sufferers of bipolar disorder experience episodes of mania that involve extremely aggressive and violent behavior.

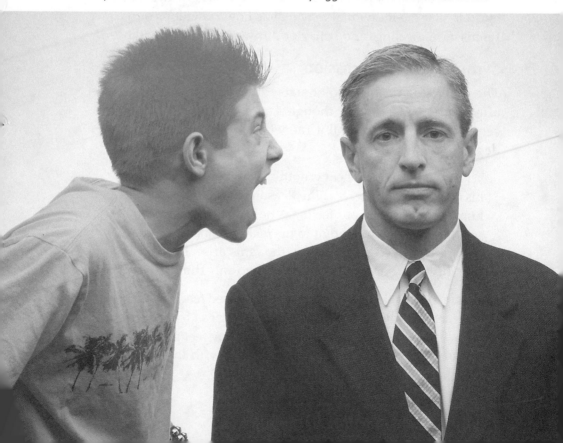

and five hundred dollars worth of knickknacks because she believed her computer had sent her a message telling her she had millions of dollars.

Other typical symptoms of mania may include increased sexual drive and indiscriminate sexual promiscuity. This often leads to divorce, pregnancy, and sexually transmitted diseases. Abuse of drugs such as cocaine, alcohol, or sleeping medications is also common during a manic state. As patients try to calm themselves or try to stay high, this drug abuse often makes the mania worse. Another symptom of mania is heightened senses, where colors seem brighter, sounds more intense, and taste and smell stronger.

All these symptoms of mania tend to go along with a denial that anything is wrong. To patients with mania, the odd sensations, intense euphoria, risky behavior, and impaired decision making do not seem unusual or out of character. Indeed, experts say that getting persons with mania to understand that something is wrong is extremely difficult, because they think their perceptions are realistic and true. It is only after a bipolar patient has finished a manic episode that the individual may realize how ridiculous or harmful his or her feelings and behavior during the episode had been.

Symptoms of Depression

The other side of the bipolar state, a depressive episode, also affects a patient's moods, thoughts, and activities. Nineteenth-century psychiatrist Emil Kraepelin aptly summed up the depressive experience:

> The patient's heart is heavy, nothing can permanently rouse his interest, nothing gives him pleasure. He has no longer any humour or any religious feeling,—he is unsatisfied with himself, has become indifferent to his relatives and to whatever he formerly liked best. Gloomy thoughts arise, his past and even his future appear to him in a uniformly dim light.[4]

As Kraepelin noted, people who are depressed feel sad and hopeless. Depression differs from normal occasional sadness, however, because it persists. Depressed people also may feel guilty, worthless, and helpless. Many become obsessed with their personal

The depressive episodes of bipolar disorder frequently involve suicidal thoughts, and many patients actually attempt to kill themselves.

Bipolar Disorder and Suicide

One of the most tragic consequences of bipolar disorder is the high risk of suicide that goes along with the disease. As many as 25 percent of patients with bipolar disorder attempt suicide, and about 10 percent succeed. By far the patients most at risk for suicide are those who abuse drugs and alcohol. This is especially true in adolescents. Substances most often used by teens who commit suicide are alcohol, stimulants such as cocaine and methamphetamine, sedatives, opiates, and marijuana.

Whether or not substance abuse is involved, the risk of suicide remains high, even for children with bipolar disorder. Those at highest risk include individuals with a history of suicide attempts, those who have recurring severe depressive episodes, those with an early onset of bipolar disorder, and those who experience irritability and agitation in the manic phase of the disease. Patients who experience major personal losses, such as a death in the family; who are socially isolated; who have co-occurring health problems; or who are homeless are also especially vulnerable to suicide.

Patients who are suicidal may or may not talk about wanting to die. They may put their finances and other assets in order and give away possessions to prepare for death. Sometimes they repeatedly put themselves in situations where they can be harmed or killed. Some people who are suicidal write a note or letter explaining their feelings and intentions. Whether or not they talk about suicide, people who reach this point are in desperate need of immediate help.

failings. Some lose the ability to enjoy anything in life. One patient described this hallmark of depression as a loss of the capacity to play or to relish any sort of beauty.

These down feelings are often accompanied by decreased energy and a feeling of tiredness or slowness. Many depressed people feel as though they are moving in slow motion and cannot find the energy to do what they need to do. Many sleep too much, while others are unable to sleep. Typically a depressed person has trouble falling asleep, awakens early, and cannot get back to sleep. Therefore, even though the individual spends a great deal of time in bed, he or she gets little sleep and feels exhausted.

Other thought and behavioral effects of depression include difficulty concentrating, remembering, and making decisions. Many depressed people describe this as a kind of mist that descends on the brain. Ordinary decisions such as what to wear or what to eat become overwhelming tasks too difficult to perform.

Changes in appetite, with weight loss or gain, also are common. Some depressed people do not feel like eating at all. Others tend to crave sweets and will binge.

Another frequent symptom of depression is chronic pain or other bodily malaise not caused by physical illness or injury. One young patient said that being depressed showed her what it meant to be old and sick, because she had constant aches and pains. Many depressed people have ongoing headaches, stomachaches, and other pains for which no physical cause can be found.

The scariest and most tragic symptoms of depression are recurring thoughts of death and suicide attempts. This is more likely to happen early during bipolar disorder, which is one reason why early identification and management of the disease is essential. Doctors say it is important for anyone who is suicidal to get immediate professional help before it is too late. The person should not be left alone or given access to weapons, drugs, or poisons that can be used to harm him- or herself.

Criteria for Mania and Depression

Many severe episodes of bipolar disorder include symptoms of psychosis. Psychosis occurs when a person no longer has a grip on reality. Some bipolar patients experience typical symptoms such as euphoria or sadness but do not lose touch with reality. Others have hallucinations and delusions, which are hallmarks of losing touch with reality. Hallucinations involve seeing, hearing, or otherwise sensing things that are not real. For example, someone who is hallucinating may see spiders in his or her bed even though there are no spiders.

After considering a patient's symptoms, doctors refer to criteria specified in a guide used by psychiatrists, called the *Diagnostic and Statistical Manual IV*, to determine if the patient is suffering from manic and depressive episodes. In diagnosing either mania or depression, doctors first make sure that symptoms are not caused by substance abuse or another medical condition, and that they cause significant distress and impairment in social or other areas of functioning. To qualify for a manic episode, a person must have an elevated mood plus three or more other typical symptoms most of the day, nearly every day, for one week or longer. Or, if the person is irritable, there must be four additional symptoms present. For a diagnosis of depression, the person must have five or more classic symptoms that last most of the day, nearly every day, for two weeks or longer.

Different Forms of the Disease

In addition to these criteria, doctors also refer to patterns of symptoms that occur in bipolar patients. These patterns enable physicians to diagnose specific people as having different forms of the disease. The most common form of the illness involves recurring episodes that alternate between mania and depression. The patient may have periods of normal mood between episodes. If a patient's first-ever episode is with mania, this tends to be the most serious and lengthy type of episode throughout the course of the illness. If the first episode involves depression, then that seems to predominate. No matter which type of episode is first, doctors refer to this form of the disorder as bipolar I disorder. It is the most severe form of the disease.

Some patients experience milder episodes of mania known as hypomania, alternating with depression. Such patients are referred

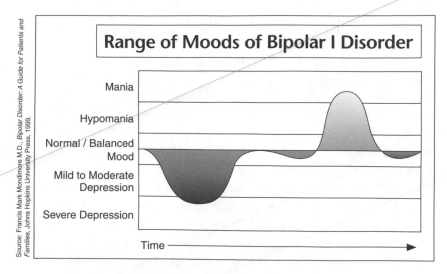

Source: Francis Mark Mondimore M.D., *Bipolar Disorder: A Guide for Patients and Families*, Johns Hopkins University Press, 1999.

to as having bipolar II disorder. This is a less severe form of the disease than is bipolar I.

Doctors also consider a form of the disease to be one in which mania and depression occur at the same time. This is known as a mixed bipolar state. Here, the individual can be energetic and agitated and have trouble sleeping, while also feeling sad and hopeless and perhaps suicidal. Psychiatrists call mixed states either agitated depression or dysphoric mania. In agitated depression, the patient is depressed but very restless, angry, or irritable. In dysphoric mania, the person is sad but displays manic activity, rushing or flailing about, screaming, or wringing their hands.

Sometimes mixed states occur when the individual is in transition from mania to depression, or vice versa; other times a mixed state may happen at random. People with mixed states generally have severe cases of manic depression. They take a long time to recover and are resistant to treatment. They are also at high risk for suicide.

Another category of bipolar disorder is rapid-cycling bipolar disorder. Doctors assign this label to patients who have bipolar I or II and experience four or more episodes of manic depression in one year. Some people with rapid cycling can have multiple episodes in a single day. Although this is unusual in adults, it can occur in children or adolescents with the disorder. Rapid cycling in adults with bipolar disorder generally involves multiple episodes over weeks or months rather than within a single day.

Many people with rapid-cycling bipolar disorder have thyroid problems that affect their metabolism. The body's metabolism refers to how the body or any living tissue burns energy. The thyroid gland in the throat produces thyroid hormone, which helps regulate the body's metabolism. Doctors do not know how thyroid problems influence rapid-cycling bipolar disorder, but they presume there is some relationship between the two.

In addition to bipolar I, bipolar II, mixed states, and rapid-cycling bipolar disorder, doctors also refer to a form of the disease called bipolar disorder not otherwise specified (NOS). This term is used for patients who do not fit into one of the other categories. For example, if a patient had manic or hypomanic episodes with no depressive episodes, he or she would be diagnosed with bipolar disorder NOS.

There are also two conditions similar to bipolar disorder that are given different names because of the severity or characteristics of the symptoms. The first is cyclothymic disorder, or cyclothymia. Doctors diagnose cyclothymic disorder when a patient experiences numerous periods of hypomania and depression that are not severe enough to qualify as bipolar disorder. Many people with cyclothymia go on to develop full-blown bipolar disorder. The second similar

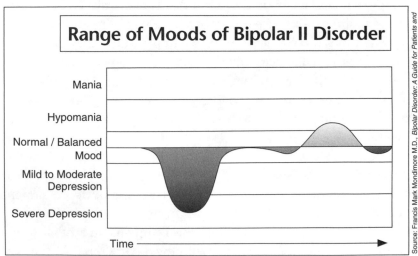

Source: Francis Mark Mondimore M.D., *Bipolar Disorder: A Guide for Patients and Families*, Johns Hopkins University Press, 1999.

disorder is schizoaffective disorder. This diagnosis is given to people who meet the criteria for bipolar disorder but who have ongoing psychotic symptoms even when the mood swings stabilize. Schizoaffective disorder is closely related to schizophrenia, a severe mental disease marked by psychotic hallucinations and delusions. However, schizoaffective disorder also includes mood abnormalities typical of bipolar disorder, which true schizophrenia does not ordinarily have.

Delays in Diagnosis

Bipolar disorder usually emerges when the patient is a young adult, yet many patients have symptoms of the disease for a long time before they see a doctor and receive a diagnosis. Some do not seek help because they believe their symptoms are due to alcohol or drug abuse or to their problems with interpersonal relationships. Others do not seek help because they do not believe they have a problem. This is especially typical of individuals in the manic phase of the disease, who feel positive and energetic. Experts call this phenomenon the seduction of mania, because the manic state seduces the individual into thinking that everything is wonderful. People in a depressive state are more likely to seek medical attention, because they feel as though everything is wrong. Still, researchers report that at least one-third of all people with bipolar disorder are not aware that they are ill and therefore do not seek a doctor's care.

James, for example, had severe ups and downs for much of his life, but only when he reached adulthood did these episodes occur so frequently and severely that he sought medical attention and was diagnosed with bipolar disorder. As he explains, "I've had times of feeling 'down' and sad most of my life. I used to skip school a lot when I felt like this because I just couldn't get out of bed. At first I didn't take these feelings very seriously. I also had times when I felt really terrific, like I could do anything. I felt really 'wound up' and I didn't need much sleep." Years later, things got worse for James: "My job was getting more stressful each week and the 'up' and 'down' times were coming more often. . . . Then, all of a sudden, I couldn't keep it together. I stopped going to work and stayed in bed for days at a time. I felt like my life wasn't worth living anymore. My wife made an appointment for me to see our family doctor."[5]

Difficulties in Diagnosis

Once a patient does decide to seek help, differentiating between the various forms of bipolar disorder and between bipolar disorder and closely related diseases is not an easy task. Because there are no physical tests such as blood tests or brain scans to determine whether someone has the disease and what form they have, diagnosis depends on a doctor's assessment of the person's medical history and symptoms over time. There is a fine line between the different forms of bipolar disorder and between bipolar disorder and related diseases such as cyclothymia and schizoaffective disorder, so sometimes this diagnosis takes time—even years—and errors in diagnosis are common. Experts estimate that up to one-third of all bipolar patients initially receive a misdiagnosis. A doctor who is a general practitioner can make a diagnosis of bipolar disorder but will usually refer a patient to a psychiatrist, a medical doctor who specializes in mental illnesses, if he or she suspects this disease. Psychiatrists have more experience in diagnosing conditions such as bipolar disorder and are therefore more likely to do this correctly.

There are several conditions that resemble bipolar disorder, preventing doctors from arriving at a correct diagnosis. People with hallucinations or delusions are likely to be diagnosed with schizophrenia. Bipolar disorder is also commonly misdiagnosed as major depression, a disorder in which a patient is severely depressed but exhibits no mania. This misdiagnosis often happens when a person has experienced depression but no mania yet. Once the patient has a manic episode, the correct diagnosis of bipolar disorder can be made. It is important that this be done correctly, because the medical treatments for major depression and bipolar disorder are very different.

Certain drugs can cause symptoms that resemble bipolar disorder, and this too may lead to an incorrect diagnosis. For example, corticosteroids used to treat a variety of autoimmune disorders and asthma can cause severe mood swings. Medications used to

Diagnosing bipolar disorder can be difficult. The doctor must check medical histories and watch symptoms over time.

treat weight problems, high blood pressure, anxiety, and Parkinson's disease can also cause mood swings that may be mistaken for bipolar disorder, as can abuse of alcohol. And cocaine and amphetamines can induce symptoms of mania and hallucinations that resemble manic episodes.

Special Problems with Diagnosis in Youth

According to mental health experts, the most difficult bipolar cases to diagnose are those that begin in children and adolescents. Some, like James, experience fairly typical bipolar symptoms but are never diagnosed because their parents do not seek help for them. Others are especially difficult to diagnose because they have atypical symptoms. Says the National Institute of Mental Health:

> Bipolar disorder is difficult to recognize and diagnose in youth because it does not fit precisely the symptom criteria established for adults, and because its symptoms can resemble or

A child psychiatrist takes notes as her patient draws. Symptoms of bipolar disorder in children are often mistaken for normal childhood emotions and behavior.

co-occur with those of other common childhood-onset mental disorders. In addition, symptoms of bipolar disorder may be initially mistaken for normal emotions and behaviors of children and adolescents.[6]

Unlike normal mood changes, however, bipolar disorder in children and adolescents severely impairs functioning in school and at home. In contrast to adults with the disorder, children and adolescents are more likely to be irritable and destructive rather than euphoric during the manic phase. This often leads to a diagnosis of attention deficit hyperactivity disorder (ADHD), oppositional defiant disorder (ODD), or conduct disorder (CD). The only way to determine if bipolar disorder rather than one of these other conditions is present is to see if manic episodes begin to alternate with depression. Also, if the child is given medication for ADHD, ODD, or CD, and the medication makes the mania worse, this is an indication that the individual has bipolar disorder rather than one of these other conditions.

During the depressive phase of bipolar disorder, children and adolescents are prone to physical complaints such as headaches, muscle aches, stomachaches, and tiredness. They frequently will be absent from school or perform poorly when they are there. They also tend to talk about running away from home, cry frequently, experience social isolation, and talk about being a failure. Sometimes it is difficult for a doctor to distinguish such symptoms of bipolar disorder from those experienced by a nonbipolar child who has few friends and is merely shy and unhappy with school.

Evidence from research on bipolar disorder indicates that children and adolescents may experience a more severe form of the illness than older teens and adults do. When bipolar disorder begins before or just after puberty, it tends to be characterized by more continuous manic and depressive episodes and to have rapid cycling rather than stable periods between episodes.

During the depressive phase of bipolar disorder, children often isolate themselves from peers and experience feelings of worthlessness and failure.

Who Has Bipolar Disorder?

People from all walks of life have bipolar disorder. It affects all social classes and does not spare anyone, no matter what their economic or employment situation. There are many famous and talented people with bipolar disorder, including astronaut Buzz Aldrin; humorist Art Buchwald; actors Ned Beatty, Patty Duke, Robert Downey Jr., Spike Milligan, Carrie Fisher, Margot Kidder, and Kristy McNichol; professional golfers John Daley and Muffin Spencer-Devlin; former professional baseball player Jim Piersall; professional football players Alonzo Spellman and Dimitrius Underwood; and writer/psychologist Kay Jamison.

All ethnic and racial groups can be affected by the disease. Statistics show that blacks and whites have approximately equal incidences of bipolar disorder, but Hispanics in the United States have a slightly lower rate of the disease for unknown reasons. The Hutterites in the United States, who live in isolated colonies, have a much-lower-than-average incidence. So do the Amish, another isolated traditionalist sect. Experts are not sure why these groups have lower rates of bipolar disorder, but they theorize it might be partially due to genetics or social factors.

Astronaut Buzz Aldrin suffers from bipolar disorder.

Who Has Bipolar Disorder?

Although diagnosis may be difficult and elusive because of similar disorders and atypical symptoms, each year doctors accurately diagnose many people with bipolar disorder. In fact, in the United States alone, there are more than 2 million people, or about 1 percent of the population, who have been diagnosed with the disease. There are probably many more who have bipolar disorder who have not yet been diagnosed.

Most cases of manic depression begin in late adolescence or early adulthood, although it can start much earlier or later in life. Even infants can have bipolar disorder, although this is rare. One infant with the disease was incredibly fussy, slept little, and screamed nonstop. As a toddler, this child could not sit still and threw violent temper tantrums, screaming, destroying things, biting, spitting, and slapping. In addition to affecting people of all ages, bipolar disorder occurs in individuals of all races, ethnic groups, and social classes. It affects an equal number of men and women, although the course of the disease varies slightly between men and women. Men are more likely to begin the disease with a manic episode, women with a depressive one. Women also are more likely to have rapid cycling.

Bipolar disorder affects a wide variety of people with varying degrees of severity. Although it is often difficult to diagnose, a correct diagnosis is essential so that the affected person can start treatment for this devastating disease.

Chapter 2

What Causes Bipolar Disorder?

O VER THE YEARS, people have argued about the causes of bipolar disorder. For example, some experts in the early twentieth century thought that bipolar disorder resulted from bad parenting, negative thinking, or overemotional reactions to stress. Other doctors believed that the disease resulted strictly from imbalances in brain biochemistry. Today, most authorities believe the disease results from a combination of causes. According to the National Institute of Mental Health, "Most scientists now agree that there is no single cause for bipolar disorder—rather, many factors act together to produce the illness."[7] These factors include genetic, biochemical, and environmental influences. Different causes may play more or less of a role for different people.

The Role of Genes

Bipolar disorder tends to run in families, so scientists have deduced that genetics is one factor that causes it. Genes, part of DNA (deoxyribonucleic acid) molecules, transmit hereditary information from parents to offspring. They are situated on worm-shaped bodies called chromosomes in the center, or nucleus, of each cell. The sequence of genes on each chromosome provides the cell containing those chromosomes with a set of instructions on how to grow and operate. A baby is born with two copies of instructions—one from each parent.

Humans have forty-six chromosomes in each cell. Twenty-three come from the mother and twenty-three from the father. The genes on each chromosome also come in pairs. In each pair, one gene comes from the mother and one from the father.

When a gene or chromosome is damaged, it results in a change called a mutation. Mutated genetic material can be passed from either the mother or the father to a child. When this occurs, the altered genetic instructions may cause various malfunctions, producing certain diseases or disorders.

Scientists have been searching for specific genes or mutations that increase a person's chances of developing bipolar disorder. They use two main types of methods in their work. One method is linkage studies, in which researchers look at particular regions of chromosomes to see if they are linked to manic-depressive illness in families in which many people have the disease. Then they analyze these regions using sophisticated chromosome-separating

Genetics researchers like this one are attempting to identify the specific genes responsible for causing bipolar disorder.

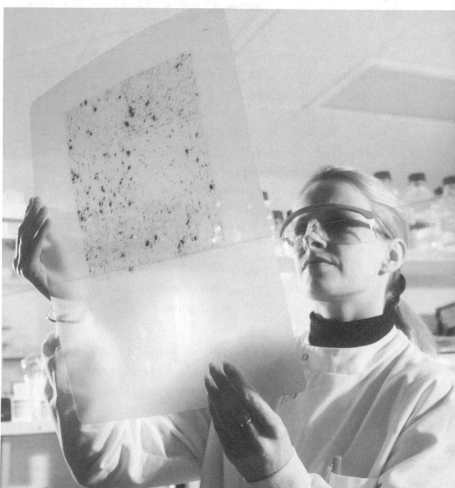

A View on Evolutionary Advantages of Bipolar Disorder

In recognizing the influence of genetic factors in causing bipolar disorder, some researchers have pointed out that having a fairly mild case of bipolar disorder might even be advantageous from an evolutionary standpoint. Genes or genetic mutations that give an advantage to a species may be selected by nature to be passed on to offspring. Some characteristics of bipolar patients may be desirable, as Samuel Barondes, the author of the book Mood Genes, *points out:*

It is, in fact, easy to make the case that the milder form of mania, called hypomania, has many adaptive aspects. With it comes optimism, enthusiasm, charisma, confidence, boldness, decisiveness, risk taking, and the uninhibited thinking that sometimes leads to creative ideas. These are attributes that are not only useful to the individuals but also attractive to others, ensuring social position and reproductive success.

This argument, of course, does not explain which genes are involved, but does offer some explanation of why certain genes have survived and continue to produce the disease. It also does not imply that the more serious forms of bipolar disorder are desirable in an evolutionary sense and therefore does not explain why such genes might continue to be transmitted by the same token.

techniques and computers. In this way, individual genes in the region can be studied to see if they are associated with the disease. So far, areas of six different chromosomes have been linked to bipolar disorder. Researchers are now looking for specific genes on these regions to determine which genes, if any, are responsible for the illness.

The other method scientists use to study genes is called association studies. With this type of research, scientists try to show that certain genes or mutations known to be related to bipolar disorder occur more frequently in individuals or families with the disease. Thus far, results have not proven anything, and no specific genes have been conclusively found to occur more frequently in people with the disease. However, scientists are reasonably sure that they will eventually find the genes responsible, because studies show that identical twins, who have identical genes, are more likely to both get bipolar disorder than are other siblings. Genes are not the whole story, however, because research has shown that the identical twin of someone with the illness does not always develop it. This indicates that genes are not the only causative factor.

Further evidence for a genetic component comes from studies showing that when one parent has the disorder, each child has a 15 to 30 percent chance of also having it. When both parents have the illness, the risk is 50 to 75 percent.

Adoption studies also indicate that genes play an important role in causing manic-depressive disorder. For example, 31 percent of adopted children with bipolar disorder have biological parents who also have the disease. This is similar to the rate of the illness among parents of children with the disease who are not adopted, which shows that genes, rather than the environment in which the child is raised, is a determining factor.

Other Biological Influences

In addition to genetics, there are other biological influences that play a role in the development of bipolar disorder. One important influence is the network of cells that make up the brain. There are about 100 billion neurons, or nerve cells, in the brain. Each neuron may be in contact with thousands of other neurons. Neurons communicate by way of neurotransmitters, or brain chemicals, and through electrical impulses. Each neuron consists of a cell body that contains a nucleus with genetic information; one or more axons, or branches that transmit signals; and multiple dendrites, or branches that receive messages on their receptors. A neuron releases neurotransmitters through its axons into a tiny gap known as a synapse. The neurotransmitter crosses the synapse and is picked up by receptors on the dendrites of the next neuron. This generates an electrical signal that is sent through the nerve cell, stimulating it to release neurotransmitters through its axons, and so on. Each neuron can receive messages from many other neurons and then pass along the message. Once a neuron releases a neurotransmitter and another neuron takes up the neurotransmitter on its receptors, the neurotransmitter can be destroyed by certain chemicals or sucked up by a pump on the neuron that produces it in a process known as reuptake.

When there are too many or not enough of certain neurotransmitters, or when there is something wrong with the way the neurotransmitters are destroyed or pumped out, this can result in a disruption of thoughts, emotions, or behavior. Scientists have studied neurotransmitters and have found that there are abnormalities that contribute to bipolar disorder. One neurotransmitter involved in bipolar disorder is dopamine. An abnormal amount of dopamine appears to underlie some of the addictive behaviors that often go along with the disorder. Dopamine influences emotional status, motor movements, learning, thinking, memory, attention, motivations, and sexual impulses. Too much dopamine can lead to mania and psychosis, and too little can induce depression, so there appears to be an imbalance of dopamine in both the manic and depressive phases of the disease.

Serotonin is another neurotransmitter scientists believe plays a role in bipolar disorder. It is well known that it influences mood. Serotonin got a lot of attention in the late 1980s when the drug Prozac was approved to treat depression. Prozac acts to increase the amount of serotonin in the brain. This neurotransmitter also plays a role in sleep and wakefulness. High levels of serotonin are associated with aggression and insufficient REM, or dream-state, sleep. Low levels of it can lead to agitation, irritability, lethargy, worrying, and suicidal behavior.

Another neurotransmitter involved in bipolar disorder is acetylcholine. It plays an important role in motor movements, thinking,

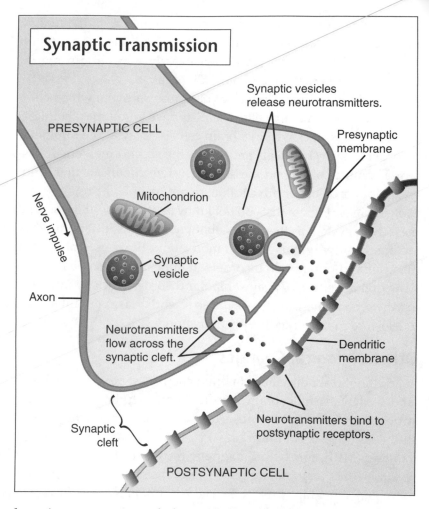

Synaptic Transmission

Synaptic vesicles release neurotransmitters.

PRESYNAPTIC CELL

Presynaptic membrane

Mitochondrion

Nerve impulse

Synaptic vesicle

Axon

Neurotransmitters flow across the synaptic cleft.

Dendritic membrane

Neurotransmitters bind to postsynaptic receptors.

Synaptic cleft

POSTSYNAPTIC CELL

learning, memory, and sleep. Norepinephrine, another neuro-transmitter, responds to stress by inducing the so-called fight-or-flight response in which the entire body is mobilized to fight or flee. The neurotransmitters glutamate and GABA (gamma aminobu-tyric acid) also appear to be involved in bipolar disorder. GABA helps prevent nerves from overfiring. Glutamate is the opposite—it is excitatory. Imbalances of these chemicals can lead to depression or mania.

Clearly, the answer to which neurotransmitters play a role in bipolar disorder is not a simple one, as scientists have determined that several contribute to the disease. The precise contribution may vary from person to person and over time within an individual, so the role of each neurotransmitter can be complicated and difficult to understand. No one yet knows exactly why certain neurotransmitters fluctuate in a given individual.

In addition to the influence of neurotransmitters, which communicate between brain cells, scientists have found that chemicals that carry messages within a brain cell also play a role in bipolar disorder. These chemicals are part of the second messenger system. Examples of second messenger system chemicals that influence bipolar disorder are choline, myo-inositol, G-proteins, and protein kinase C. Scientists do not know as much about the second messenger system as they know about neurotransmitters, but they are busy studying it to find out more about the causes of bipolar disorder and other brain disorders. It appears that some medications that are effective against bipolar disorder work by influencing the second messenger system, so scientists are very interested in learning more about this phenomenon.

Other Biological Changes

In addition to abnormalities in brain chemicals, people with bipolar disorder have other brain abnormalities, including altered brain structure and function. Scientists use several imaging techniques to study these aspects of the brain. They include magnetic resonance imaging (MRI), functional magnetic resonance imaging (fMRI), positron emission tomography (PET), and single photon emission computed tomography (SPECT). These techniques allow doctors to take pictures of the structures and activities inside the brain.

Although researchers have not yet proven that changes in the structure and function of the brain cause bipolar disorder, they have found that such changes do occur when the disease develops and hypothesize that these changes are likely to be responsible for at least some aspects of the disease. Using MRI scans, scientists have found that the spaces between the folds of the brain, known as the cortical sulci, are enlarged in bipolar patients. The canals known as the cerebral ventricles, which carry cerebrospinal fluid (the liquid that encases the brain and spinal cord) through the brain, are also enlarged in persons with bipolar disorder. These areas are

High-Tech Imaging Techniques for Probing the Brain

Doctors use several high-tech brain imaging techniques to assess brain changes that occur in bipolar disorder. MRI uses a magnetic field and radio waves to create images of the inside of the body. An MRI machine is a large, cylindrical magnetic tube. When a person is placed inside the machine, radio waves produced by a coil in the machine cause the body to emit faint signals. The machine picks up these signals and processes them through a computer, which creates corresponding images from the person's insides. Specially trained doctors can then analyze certain body tissues by the electronic characteristics they display.

fMRI is a technique for assessing the parts of the brain that are activated by different physical sensations or activities. This can tell scientists which parts of the brain are active during a bipolar episode. An MRI scan is set up so that the increased blood flow to an area activated by stimulation shows up on the scan. Stimulation is delivered to the person inside the magnetic tube or as the person performs a particular activity, and MRI scans are taken to see which parts of the brain respond.

A PET scan is an imaging technique that uses positively charged particles to detect changes in the chemical activities in the body. This enables doctors to assess which brain chemicals are active or deficient in bipolar disorder. It provides a color-coded image of certain functions. The patient receives a tracer either by injection into a vein or by inhalation. The tracer emits positrons, or positively charged particles, which collide with electrons, or negatively charged particles, to emit gamma rays. The PET scanner detects these gamma rays and forwards the results to a computer, which analyzes the functions of the organ being targeted.

SPECT works in a similar manner to PET and is used to examine the function of certain regions of the brain. With SPECT, the patient is injected with a radioactive tracer linked to chemicals that show up in the brain. The SPECT machine monitors photons, or light packets, emitted from the tracer as it is carried in the blood to the brain. All of these techniques enable doctors to learn more about the brain activity of patients with bipolar disorder.

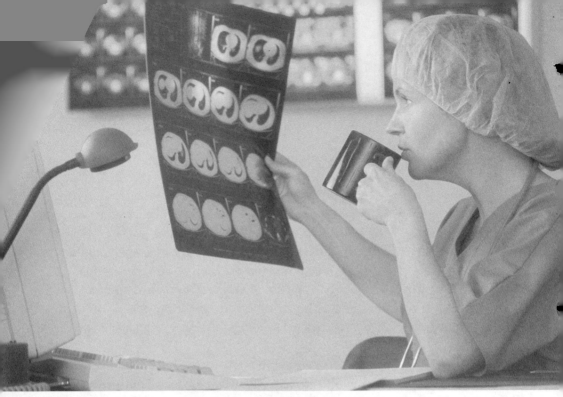

Doctors study MRI images like this one in order to learn more about the brain activity of their patients with bipolar disorder.

18 to 20 percent larger in patients with bipolar disorder than in healthy people. In identical twins, when one twin has manic-depressive disorder and the other does not, only the twin with bipolar disorder has enlarged cortical sulci and cerebral ventricles. This is compelling evidence that there is a correlation between these changes and the disease. In addition, in a recent study one medication used to treat bipolar disorder decreased the volume of the cerebral ventricles. This finding offers more evidence that the size of these areas is a causative factor.

Other research using PET scans and MRI studies have found abnormal brain activity in several areas of the brain during manic and depressive episodes. These areas, which include the prefrontal cortex, basal ganglia, and temporal lobe regions, are important in regulating mood and logical connections between language and memory. Scientists do not yet know whether this abnormal brain activity causes or results from bipolar disorder.

MRI studies have also revealed that the brains of people with bipolar disorder have lesions, or abnormal areas of destruction, in the white matter. The white matter is composed of nerve cell fibers encased in fatty sheaths that are white in color. These sheaths help to transmit electrical impulses in the brain. The lesions in people with bipolar disorder tend to be concentrated in areas of the brain that perform emotional processing. These types of lesions also can occur in healthy people and normally increase in frequency as people age, but they appear far more often than expected in young people with bipolar disorder. However, not all patients with the disease have lesions. This indicates that lesions may or may not contribute to the development of the disease. More research is needed to determine a causative role, if any.

Other Body Systems

In addition to a link between abnormalities in the brain and bipolar disorder, there is evidence that malfunctions in other body systems may contribute to the disease. One system that appears to play a role is the endocrine system. The endocrine system involves glands that produce hormones of various types. The thyroid gland and the HPA axis (hypothalamic-pituitary-adrenal system) have been the primary areas of the endocrine system related to bipolar disorder. The hypothalamus is an area of the brain that regulates many endocrine functions. The pituitary gland secretes growth hormone, and the adrenal glands above the kidneys secrete cortisol, a stress hormone. All these areas seem to be related to bipolar disorder. The hypothalamus releases chemicals that cause these glands to secrete certain hormones. If the hypothalamus or any of these glands are disrupted or diseased, severe mood disorders can result. For example, when the thyroid gland does not produce enough thyroid hormone, severe depression may result. On the other hand, an overactive thyroid gland can cause high energy levels and euphoria. While researchers have found that levels of various chemicals in the hypothalamus and of various hormones are abnormal in people with bipolar disorder, they still have not yet proven that these abnormalities actually cause the disorder or simply result from it.

Disruption in body rhythms may also play a causative role in bipolar disorder. Systems in the brain and the rest of the body govern cycles

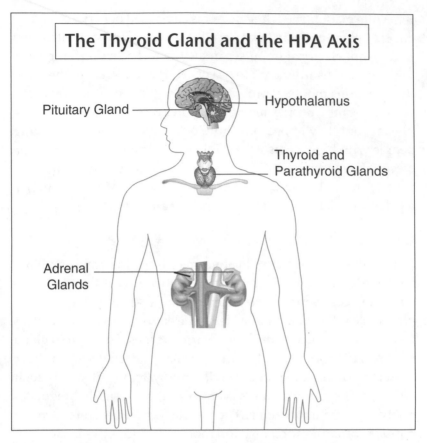

The Thyroid Gland and the HPA Axis

Pituitary Gland

Hypothalamus

Thyroid and
Parathyroid Glands

Adrenal
Glands

of sleep and wakefulness and seasonal fluctuations in various chemicals. The cyclic nature of the disease has led to a great deal of research on this topic, because "manic depressive illness is, by definition, a disturbance of rhythms."[8] Not only does the disease occur in cycles, but mania occurs more commonly during the summer and suicide more commonly during the spring and fall. Mania and depression also cause severe disruptions to a person's sleep-wake cycles, which are an important part of biorhythms.

Although there has been a great deal of research connecting body rhythms to bipolar disorder, no one has yet proven that disruptions in this body system cause the disease. Many experts believe that biorhythms most likely do play an important causative role, but researchers have yet to prove how this system works to produce the disease.

Environmental Factors

While there are various biological causes of bipolar disorder, there are also environmental triggers linked to the disease. Some experts believe that severe stresses in childhood change the chemistry of the brain so that manic-depressive disease develops later on. This is known as the kindling-stress model of causation. Researchers Robert Post and Susan Weiss formulated the kindling-stress model based on the principle that when a fire is ignited by kindling, a series of small flames suddenly bursts into a large flame when a critical temperature is reached. These researchers believe that in some people many stressors added together finally produce a full-blown case of bipolar disorder.

Extensive research has focused on sexual and psychological abuse and the early loss of a parent as possible stressors responsible for bipolar disorder, but results have been mixed. Some studies show a link between such stressors and the later development of the disease, while others show no increase in the incidence of bipolar disorder after such

An abused child cowers on the floor with her teddy bear. Some studies link childhood abuse with the onset of bipolar disorder later in life.

stressors. Despite the lack of proof, however, many mental health authorities strongly believe that these types of stressors are a primary cause for manic-depressive illness. Such authorities point out that the kindling-stress model is consistent with animal studies that show that severe stress alters the production of neurotransmitters and the second messenger system within a nerve cell. Stress also affects certain hormones, such as cortisol, that are known to play a role in the development of bipolar disorder. The kindling-stress theory supports the finding that some individuals have a genetic predisposition to be more sensitive to stress and to respond to it by developing bipolar disorder. Ray, a patient with bipolar disorder, had lifelong difficulties dealing with stressors. He responded to stressful situations by entering a bipolar episode. If he started or ended a relationship with a woman, he would immediately go into a manic or depressive state. Only after he received proper treatment with medication did the episodes come under control.

Infectious Agents

Another environmental cause for bipolar disorder that has been widely studied is infectious agents. Recent research shows that the blood of many people with bipolar disorder has antibodies to the Borna disease virus. Antibodies are molecules created by the body's immune system in response to exposure to a particular antigen, or foreign substance. The Borna disease virus causes serious central nervous system injuries in animals, which lead to behavior similar to human bipolar disorder. It does not seem to produce such dramatic effects when it infects humans, but scientists hypothesize that when it is transmitted to humans through the saliva of infected animals, it can lead to the development of severe psychiatric disorders, including bipolar disorder.

Other studies have indicated that the blood of pregnant women who gave birth to children who later developed bipolar disorder had increased levels of antibodies to taxoplasmosis, a parasite carried by cats. This is another infectious agent that scientists believe may play a role in causing bipolar disorder.

Causes Versus Risk Factors

In discussing the causes of manic-depressive illness, experts generally distinguish between actual causes and risk factors. "I' tinction, however, is not always clear. Genetics, stress, and certain infectious agents, for example, are considered to be actual causes, even though no one has conclusively proven that any of these cause the disease. Risk factors, on the other hand, are linked to bipolar disorder but are not considered by experts to play a causative role. These include winter birth, summer onset of mania, pregnancy and birth complications, and social class. Because being born during the winter months increases an individual's chances of developing bipolar disorder, this is considered to be a risk factor. Researchers have found this to be true consistently in large studies throughout the world. No one is sure why this factor influences the development of the disease, but experts hypothesize that it may have something to do with seasonal variations in pregnancy and birth complications, amount of daylight, toxins, nutritional factors, infectious agents, and weather.

The summer onset risk factor means that the summer months are a more common time for the development of mania. Doctors

Babies born during the winter months are at greater risk for developing bipolar disorder. Scientists are uncertain why winter birth represents a risk factor.

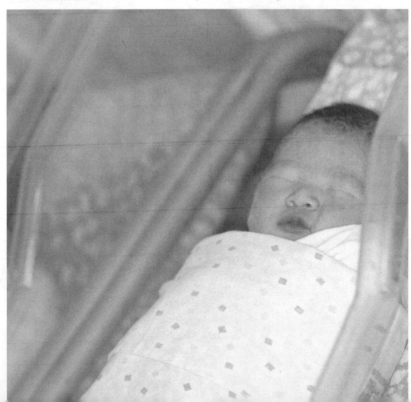

in Europe noticed this two hundred years ago, and in the 1970s researchers became interested in finding out more about the phenomenon. Several large studies have since documented that significantly more people develop mania in the summer as compared to the rest of the year. This occurs in both the Northern and Southern hemispheres, where the seasons are reversed. No one is sure why this occurs, but some experts believe that seasonal fluctuations in certain body chemicals that influence the brain may play a role.

Many studies have found that babies whose mothers experience pregnancy and birth complications have a higher risk of developing bipolar disorder later in life. Again, the reason for this higher risk is unknown and may have something to do with infections or other factors.

Other studies have found that bipolar disorder affects the higher social classes more than it affects the lower ones, so this is another documented risk factor for the disease. Some experts have suggested that personality traits associated with the disorder may lead to economic and social success. Others have hypothesized that certain stressors of living in a higher social class may help trigger the disease. None of these theories has been proven.

By looking at both risk factors and causes of bipolar disorder, it is apparent that there is no simple answer to what causes and predisposes people to the disease. Instead, there appears to be a complex set of biological and environmental factors that play a role, and different factors may be more or less influential for different people.

Chapter 3

How Is Bipolar Disorder Treated?

According to the National Institute of Mental Health, "Most people with bipolar disorder—even those with the most severe forms—can achieve substantial stabilization of their mood swings and related symptoms with proper treatment."[9] Because the disease recurs in cycles, experts recommend that treatment be given on an ongoing basis rather than just in response to specific episodes. This treatment ideally consists of medication and psychological therapy.

Even with continuous treatment, patients will still experience some drastic mood changes. Doctors say that a bipolar patient should always keep the physician informed about any such changes. That way, the doctor can adjust the treatment plan to help avert extreme mood swings.

Lack of Treatment

While many patients who receive proper, ongoing treatment do well and are able to live fairly normal lives, mental health authorities say that a big problem with bipolar disorder is that so many patients do not receive treatment at all. Nearly half the people with bipolar disorder in the United States are not receiving any sort of treatment. This may be for several reasons. One reason is that people who are not experiencing symptoms may stop taking medication. Other people lack health insurance to pay for mental health care and are not treated because of the prohibitive expense of such care. Still others are afraid to seek treatment because doing so would be admitting that they have a mental disease. This

Some people with bipolar disorder refuse to seek proper treatment fearing they may be stigmatized for having a mental illness.

may be frightening to individuals because they are afraid of what others will think or that they will lose their jobs because they are mentally ill. Many people are afraid of taking medicine because of the inconvenience and side effects and so do not seek treatment for that reason.

By far the most prevalent reason people with bipolar disorder do not seek treatment is because they do not think they need it. This is usually because they do not understand that they have a mental illness. In such cases, a family member or friend may take the person to a doctor or mental health clinic for an evaluation. But if the individual is not considered to be a threat to him- or herself or to others, by law no one can force him or her to seek treatment. If the person is a threat or commits a crime, law enforcement officials can order hospitalization and treatment against the person's will. There are some people and civil liberties groups that argue that medicating people against their will is unjust and infringes on their right to privacy. However, many mental health experts point out that, in many cases, forcing treatment is best for the individual and for others:

> What these well-meaning but misguided advocates have failed to understand is that approximately one-third of all individuals with manic depression have little awareness of their illness. When such individuals refuse medication they are doing so as a result of illogical or irrational thought processes. The right to be free of the symptoms of a brain disease must be weighed against the individual's right to privacy. . . . The right to privacy must also be weighed against the needs of the patient's family and society as a whole, especially in cases involving individuals who become assaultive or violent when not taking medications.[10]

Add this to the fact that without treatment, bipolar disorder leads to suicide in 20 percent of cases and often leads to homelessness, and the argument for forcing treatment becomes stronger. For example, experts estimate that there are about twenty-five thousand people in the United States who are homeless because they refuse to take medication that could control their symptoms of mental illness. Many who do not accept treatment also end up committing

Many patients who refuse medication to control the symptoms of the illness end up homeless like this man.

crimes and getting arrested over and over again. One woman with untreated bipolar disorder was arrested forty-nine times in five years; one man was in jail thirty-five times and hospitalized twenty times, but he refused to take medication on an ongoing basis.

Beginning Treatment

Ideally, of course, a person with bipolar disorder accepts the need for treatment and complies with a doctor's orders. This helps avoid some of the unpleasant and difficult issues involved in forcible treatment.

When a person with bipolar disorder does decide to seek treatment, the first step toward success is choosing a good doctor, preferably a psychiatrist, or specialist in mental disorders. Experts say the doctor should be up-to-date on current information and therapy and should be accessible to the patient at reasonable times. Most patients with bipolar disorder can begin treatment on an outpatient basis, as long as they are willing to report back regularly to the doctor, but hospitalization may be required to stabilize severe cases, especially if patients are suicidal or out of control.

A patient can be hospitalized in a special psychiatric hospital or in the psychiatric ward of a general hospital. The purpose of hospitalization is to get the symptoms under control so the individual can function on his or her own. This entails trying various medications and combinations of medications until the right one works. It may also involve physically restraining the person if he or she is violent or likely to harm him- or herself or others. Most patients do not like being in the hospital, but many realize that it is necessary to get their condition under control. Hospitalization can last anywhere from a few days to years, depending on how quickly a successful treatment is found.

Mood Stabilizers

Once a patient is under the care of a doctor, treatment begins with getting the person on medication, which is the primary weapon against bipolar disorder. According to the authors of *Surviving Manic Depression,* "Medications are the single most important aspect of the treatment of manic-depressive illness. Medication treatment has two main goals: first to alleviate or shorten the duration of an acute episode of mania, hypomania, or depression, and second, to maintain the improvement obtained in the acute phase and prevent further cycles of mania or depression."[11]

Drugs that patients take on a long-term basis to stabilize moods and prevent acute episodes of mania and depression are known as mood stabilizers. There are several types of mood stabilizers. Lithium, the primary mood stabilizer in use, was the first one approved by the U.S. Food and Drug Administration (FDA) to treat bipolar disorder. The effects of lithium were first documented by psychiatrist John Cade in 1949 in

Victoria, Australia. While studying the breakdown of proteins from the urine of patients with manic-depressive illness, Cade discovered that injecting lithium into guinea pigs calmed the animals. He then tested lithium on a group of patients with bipolar disorder, and most experienced a dramatic recovery. But his discovery remained relatively unknown for some time, and it was not until twenty years later that lithium was approved for clinical use in the United States.

Since lithium was approved for use, it has been the mood stabilizer of choice to treat bipolar disorder. But because it takes a few days to a few weeks to become effective, it is usually combined with faster-acting drugs to treat acute mania. Once it starts working, lithium is effective in treating mania and depression. It is also good for long-term use to prevent episodes of mania and depression in many patients. It reduces the severity of episodes that occur in relapsed cases and also reduces the frequency of relapses in about two-thirds of the patients who are treated with it.

While lithium helps many patients, it is ineffective for others, and doctors have learned that several factors are useful in predicting who will and will not have a positive response. People who generally experience good results have a typical case of bipolar disorder with no mixed states, no schizoaffective disorder, and no rapid cycling.

How Is Lithium Given?

Lithium is given in the form of tablets or as a liquid. It is generally taken twice a day. Most patients take 600 to 1,200 milligrams (mg) per day. There are two extended-release tablet forms of the drug that release it more uniformly throughout the day and night. This helps keep a more even concentration of lithium in the brain.

Before a doctor starts a patient on lithium, he or she will perform blood tests to make sure the patient's kidneys are healthy enough to withstand the drug, as it can be toxic. These tests should be repeated every six to twelve months while the person is taking lithium. In addition, experts recommend that patients receive blood tests to check the level of lithium in the blood. These tests should be frequent when the person first starts the drug and every three to six months thereafter. Testing for blood levels of lithium helps guard against toxicity and adverse side effects.

Dr. John Cade and Lithium

Many medical historians regard Dr. John Cade's discovery of the effectiveness of lithium in treating bipolar disorder as one of the major twentieth-century advances in psychiatry. Yet at the time of his discovery, Cade was a medical officer working in a makeshift laboratory in a converted wooden shed on the grounds of a war veteran's hospital outside Melbourne, Australia.

Cade became interested in running experiments on the underlying causes of bipolar disorder while being held for three years as a prisoner of war in the Changi prisoner-of-war camp in Singapore. While there, Cade was allowed to practice medicine, and he discovered in postmortem autopsies on his patients with manic-depressive illness that all had brain abnormalities. This led him to hypothesize that there was an underlying physical cause for the illness. When he returned to Australia, he began conducting experiments to search for a likely toxic agent in the urine of his patients with bipolar disorder.

By injecting guinea pigs with the urine of his patients and of healthy people, he was able to find out that there was something in the urea, a chemical component of urine, that was toxic. He then began testing compounds that could modify this toxicity and found that the chemical lithium urate worked well. He then tried lithium carbonate to assess whether the lithium was responsible for the detoxification and found that the lithium carbonate caused the animals to become very lethargic. He then tested the compound on his manic patients with positive results.

In addition to the potential for damaging the kidneys, lithium can impair the function of the thyroid gland. The drug also can create a host of other dangerous and unpleasant side effects. One common side effect is a tremor of the hands known as postural tremor. The tremor is most evident when the arms are held still. If this occurs, lowering the dose of lithium may help; if this does not help, another mood-stabilizing drug may have to be used.

Lithium also may impair coordination, particularly soon after a patient begins taking it. Athletes, musicians, and others who require a high degree of motor coordination in particular may notice this side effect. The drug also can impair memory and concentration, and it can affect the heart's rhythm. Skin rashes are a common side effect, along with psoriasis, an inflammation of the skin. Some patients complain of hair loss or changes in the texture of the hair. As many as 25 percent of patients on lithium gain weight, perhaps as much as ten pounds or more. This can be a problem for those who are already overweight or for those with a medical condition made worse by weight gain. Lithium also can irritate the stomach and intestines and produce nausea or diarrhea.

Patients taking lithium as a mood stabilizer must have their blood tested regularly in order to prevent a toxic buildup of the drug in their systems.

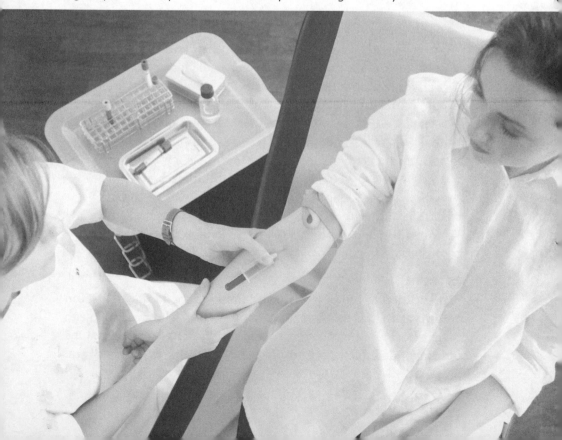

Other Mood Stabilizers

When lithium cannot be tolerated or does not work, doctors may prescribe one of two other mood stabilizers: valproate and carbamazepine. Valproate (marketed as Depakote or Depakene) is an anticonvulsant often used as a mood stabilizer. It was first used to treat epilepsy, a seizure disorder, and later used to treat bipolar disorder. It is very effective in treating acute mania in many cases and seems to begin working faster than lithium does. It is more effective than lithium in patients with rapid cycling or mixed states. However, it is not effective in treating depressive episodes, so in this respect it has a disadvantage compared with lithium.

Valproate can be taken in tablet, capsule, or syrup form. Most patients take 500 to 3,000 mg per day. Because the drug can cause liver damage and a decrease in the number of blood platelets, physicians do blood tests to check these factors every three to six months during treatment. They check also for blood levels of valproate to make sure a therapeutic level is maintained, as too much valproate in the blood can be toxic.

There are usually fewer side effects from valproate than from lithium, although many patients still experience adverse effects. The most common is nausea. Others are sleepiness, decreased concentration, hair loss, weight gain, and mild tremors. In addition, long-term use of valproate has been associated with ovarian cysts in women.

Carbamazepine, marketed as Tegretol, is the other mood stabilizer often used to treat bipolar disorder. Like valproate, it was originally developed as a medication to treat epilepsy. When doctors noticed that it improved the mood of patients with epilepsy, it was tested as a treatment for manic-depressive illness.

Carbamazepine is effective in treating acute mania and depression in about 60 percent of patients. It is more effective than lithium for cases involving mixed states and rapid cycling. The drug is available as a tablet, chewable tablet, capsule, or liquid. It is taken three to four times per day, except for the sustained-release capsules, which are taken twice per day.

Blood tests are taken every three to six months to make sure carbamazepine is not causing liver damage or a decrease in white blood cells and platelets. The drug also can cause other side effects that often make patients stop taking it. Early on in treatment, it may cause dizziness, sleepiness, and headache. In elderly patients it sometimes causes confusion and abnormal heart rhythms. It impairs the body's ability to balance salt and fluid and may thus cause swelling of the ankles. About 10 percent of people who take it experience allergic skin reactions, which require stopping treatment with the drug. Nausea is another common side effect. Because carbamazepine also can interact adversely with other medications, many doctors are hesitant about prescribing it for bipolar disorder, and it is used less frequently than are lithium and valproate.

Other Medications

In addition to the mood stabilizers that most patients with bipolar disorder must take, many need other medications to treat their illness and the problems that go along with it. Many patients use antidepressants in addition to mood stabilizers to treat the depressive phase of their illness. These may include fluoxetine (Prozac), sertraline (Zoloft), paroxetine (Paxil), or one of several other drugs.

Besides antidepressants, some patients with bipolar disorder also need antipsychotic medication. These patients have delusions, hallucinations, or other thought disruptions. Drugs used to treat such psychotic symptoms are called antipsychotics. There are two main types: conventional and atypical. Conventional, or older, antipsychotics include fluphenazine (Prolixin), haloperidol (Haldol), and chlorpromazine (Thorazine). Atypical, or newer, antipsychotics include clozapine (Clozaril), risperidone (Risperdal), and olanzapine (Zyprexa). The main drawback of these drugs is that they produce movement problems such as tremors, stiffness, and muscle spasms.

Special Problems for Pregnant Women

All the drugs used to treat bipolar disorder can pose problems and risks for pregnant women, as they can harm a developing fetus. Lithium, for example, can lead to heart abnormalities and is linked to decreased muscle tone at birth, abnormal thyroid function, and abnormal kidney function. For these reasons, doctors recommend that

Common Medications for Bipolar Disorder

Mood Stabilizers

Generic Name:	Trade Name:
lithium	Eskalith CR, Lithobid
valproate	Depakote, Depakene
carbamazepine	Tegretol

Antidepressants

Generic Name:	Trade Name:
fluoxetine	Prozac
sertraline	Zoloft
paroxetine	Paxil

Antipsychotics

Generic Name:	Trade Name:
fluphenazine	Prolixin
haloperidol	Haldol
chlorpromazine	Thorazine
clozapine	Clozaril
risperidone	Risperdal
olanzapine	Zyprexa

women with bipolar disorder who plan to become pregnant gradually taper off and discontinue taking lithium prior to pregnancy.

Anticonvulsants used to treat bipolar disorder also can cause birth defects. They are associated with spina bifida, a condition in which the spinal column does not develop normally, and other defects. Experts recommend that pregnant women not take these medications.

Psychotherapy

In addition to medication, certain forms of psychotherapy also are helpful in treating many people with bipolar disorder. In psychotherapy the patient talks with and/or practices various behaviors with a therapist. A licensed psychologist, social worker, or counselor provides this type of treatment. According to experts, "Studies have confirmed that psychotherapy helps stabilize moods and reduces the need for hospitalization. In addition, psychotherapy can improve your relationships and help you function better in many areas of your life."[12]

One type of psychotherapy often used to treat bipolar disorder is called cognitive behavioral therapy (CBT). Here, a therapist helps the patient learn to change inappropriate or negative thought patterns and behaviors to positive ones. This type of therapy has been shown to help patients function better and make them more responsible about taking their medication. Cognitive behavioral therapy combines two types of psychotherapy: cognitive therapy and behavioral therapy. Cognitive therapy attempts to teach a patient how certain thinking patterns cause disruptions in emotions and lifestyle. When patients change these thinking patterns, their trou-

Cognitive behavioral psychotherapy can help people with bipolar disorder alter their destructive behaviors and manic-depressive thought patterns.

blesome symptoms can be alleviated. According to one bipolar patient: "I found CBT to be effective in helping change the negative thinkings that go along with depression. It is not too difficult to learn to use."[13] Behavioral therapy helps patients change habitual behaviors that are a response to stressful situations. It also teaches them methods to calm the mind and body.

Another type of useful psychotherapy is psychoeducation. This involves teaching patients and their families about the illness and its treatments. This way, the patient and family members can become aware of early signs that an episode is beginning and can seek medical attention before the episode becomes full blown. In psychoeducation, patients and family members learn to evaluate and understand exactly what occurs during acute manic and depressive episodes in an effort to prevent these incidents from getting out of control. It also aims to motivate patients to take prescribed medications and to avoid alcohol and drug abuse. Studies have shown that this form of therapy helps patients and families develop coping skills and decreases relapses.

Family therapy also involves the patient and family. A therapist treats the entire family to try to reduce the stress that may contribute to or result from the bipolar disorder. This form of therapy works on improving communication and problem-solving skills within the family. It also teaches the family to accept the loved one's illness and to be supportive while not stifling the patient. Often a family is fearful of what will happen during the next manic or depressive episode, and this type of therapy can help them learn to deal with the stress. Studies show that family therapy is helpful in motivating the patient to take his or her medication and in helping to avoid rehospitalization.

Interpersonal and social rhythm therapy (IPSRT) helps patients to improve relationships with others and to stabilize a daily routine. Daily routines and regular sleep schedules help protect against manic and depressive episodes. In IPSRT, patients track their mood states and activities each day. They also write down an inventory of their social contacts, including any conflicts and stresses that occur to upset their daily rhythm and emotional stability. The therapist helps the patient learn to minimize these conflicts and to optimally stabilize daily rhythms. Studies show that IPSRT helps patients recover from episodes more quickly and achieve more stability in their daily lives. One study in particular found that IPSRT combined with drug therapy did a better job of keeping patients free of depressive episodes than did drug therapy alone. According to a researcher in the study, "Clearly, there is a benefit to using interpersonal and social rhythm therapy as part of a long-term treatment plan. Our results show that it is possible for people with bipolar disorder to have a much better quality of life."[14]

In addition to these formal types of psychotherapy, experts also recommend a variety of stress reduction techniques that can decrease the relapse rate for manic-depressive episodes. One method of reducing stress is regular exercise. Exercise reduces muscle tension and increases the brain's production of endorphins, which elevate mood. Studies have shown that regular exercise improves the mood when bipolar patients are depressed and calms them when they are manic.

Another method of stress reduction is relaxation techniques such as meditation, yoga, and massage. These have been shown to help bipolar patients remain stable.

Regular exercise reduces stress levels, which can help patients better control their disorder.

Bipolar Disorder and Nutritional Supplements

Many dietary supplement manufacturers have claimed that certain supplements are therapeutic for bipolar disorder. This has led many people with the illness to try a variety of supplements in hopes of getting relief without taking medication. But doctors caution that the value of these supplements is unproven and that patients should never discontinue their prescribed medications in order to try these substances. It is also not a good idea to use such supplements in combination with prescription medications, because they may interact adversely. Doctors advise patients to check with their physicians before adding any supplements to their regimen.

Some of the supplements that manufacturers and others have claimed are helpful for bipolar disorder include substances that help to raise serotonin levels, such as L-tryptophan, 5-hydroxytryptophan (HTP), and S-adenosylmethionine (SAMe). Folic acid and vitamin B[7], known to play a role in the production of neurotransmitters, have also been recommended, along with vitamin C, which supposedly rids the body of vanadium, a chemical linked to the development of bipolar disorder. Choline, a supplement that is supposed to increase the brain levels of the neurotransmitter acetylcholine, and inositol, a chemical that some practitioners claim decreases depression, are others that have been touted. In addition, some people claim that the herbs St. John's wort, kava, ginkgo biloba, and valerian have positive effects, although there is little scientific evidence to prove these claims.

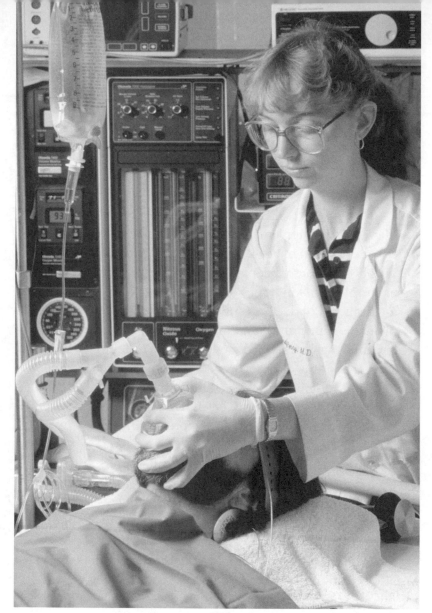

An anesthesiologist administers ether to an electroconvulsive therapy patient. Although riskier than other treatments for bipolar disorder, ECT can be effective.

When Medication and Psychotherapy Fail

In cases where medication and psychotherapy are ineffective in treating bipolar disorder, doctors may use electroconvulsive therapy (ECT). ECT also is used in situations where medication can be dangerous, such as in pregnant women, as doctors have determined that ECT does not harm the fetus.

With ECT, electrodes are taped to the patient's head. The person is anesthetized and given a muscle relaxant. Then an electrical current is passed through the brain for less than a second. This produces a brain seizure and affects blood flow and the metabolism of neurotransmitters within the brain. Usually, after several treatments, symptoms subside. ECT is generally given three times a week for six to twelve weeks.

ECT is effective for treating severe depression, mania, or mixed episodes. A serious side effect in some patients is loss of memory, but experts say that usually modern ECT techniques manage to avoid this risk. Many people are wary of taking ECT treatments, fearing that they are cruel and inhumane. But most doctors say that modern improvements in anesthesia and in the ECT technique itself have made the procedure safer than it used to be and effective in about 75 percent of bipolar patients who receive the treatment. For those who are not helped by medication or psychotherapy, the risks involved with ECT are often worth taking in order to bring bipolar disorder under some sort of control.

The Cost of Treatment

The cost of bipolar treatment—whether it involves medication, psychotherapy, or ECT—is very expensive, even when a patient is covered by medical insurance. For those patients who do not have insurance, some are eligible for Medicaid benefits from the government. Those who are disabled from the disease and cannot work may qualify for government assistance programs. These programs, however, do not come close to covering the costs associated with treatment, and this continues to be a burden for many families affected by the disease.

Despite the tremendous expenses involved, modern treatments for bipolar disorder are successful in controlling the disease in many patients. This represents true progress, as even just a few decades ago there was nothing that could be done for people suffering from manic-depressive illness.

Chapter 4

Living with Bipolar Disorder

Even when controlled with medication, bipolar disorder involves trauma and disruptions that impact every aspect of a patient's life. As the author of *Bipolar Disorder Demystified* states it,

> Living with bipolar disorder is much like living your life on a tightrope—not because you choose to walk that tightrope but because it's the only available surface upon which you can walk. One false step, one impulsive moment, could easily end your life. Imagine being destined to walk that rope forever—either romping ecstatically across it or fighting a force that's pulling you down, and rarely achieving that elusive level ground. This is the experience of bipolar disorder.[15]

For most people with bipolar disorder, the balancing act begins long before a diagnosis is made, even though they are unaware of what is wrong. Then, once they are diagnosed, the ride gets a little smoother as treatment begins and symptoms subside, although this does not always happen. Some patients refuse to accept the diagnosis and do nothing to try to get better. Ginny, for example, who was diagnosed as a teen, recalls, "My initial response to my diagnosis was 'Oh no, not me! There must be another explanation for my behavior and mood swings, I'm not mentally ill!' I began seeking other doctors hoping for another explanation. Consequently, I spent more than a year in denial trying to cover up my pain. Fortunately, I found a caring therapist. She helped me to see reality for what it is."[16]

Unlike Ginny, though, many patients are happy to receive a definitive diagnosis. James, who suffered severe mood swings for many years before going to a doctor, was relieved when he finally got a diagnosis. He felt that finally, now that his condition had a name, he could begin treatment and hopefully get better. Becky, a college student, also felt that the correct diagnosis helped point her life in the right direction:

> I had been treated for depression since adolescence, but at college a doctor diagnosed me with bipolar II disorder, and strangely enough, just having this diagnosis started turning things around for me. I had an answer to why I felt the way I did, why I did some of the things I did. It made me feel that maybe I wasn't some horrible, faulted individual but someone who had a serious, valid medical illness. Since then, I have started turning myself around.[17]

Disruptions in Everyday Life While Adjusting Treatment

No matter how relieved or positive an individual feels about a diagnosis, the fact remains that having bipolar disorder causes major life disruptions and challenges even with successful

A woman discusses her condition with a psychologist. For patients with bipolar disorder, effective treatment begins with a definitive diagnosis.

Many patients with bipolar disorder abuse alcohol, which can intensify feelings of aggression during the manic phase and lead to violent behavior.

treatment. For one thing, finding the right combination of medications to control the condition may take time, sometimes as much as several years. During this time, some patients must drop out of school, quit work, or otherwise stop their normal activities. Murray, for example, was an outstanding student and athlete in high school, but soon after graduation his plans to go on to college and become a professional athlete were shattered when he had his first bipolar episode. He was hospitalized and put on medication, which made him sick, and he had to give up his university scholarship. It took about three years before his condition stabilized and he was able to begin school again.

Angel, who has had bipolar disorder since childhood but was not diagnosed until she was in her thirties, also had difficulties with medication and subsequent disruptions of her life. "I have gone through several medications to find the correct one. In the meantime, relationships and lifestyle have been extremely difficult for me. I have been in the hospital three times. I probably needed to be there more often. Employment has been almost impossible for me to maintain."[18] One reason why many patients such as Angel experience difficulties with relationships and everyday life is that the behavior of a person with bipolar disorder can become intolerable. Many people in the manic phase, for example, spend ridiculous sums of money, which can deplete bank accounts and cause strife within a family. Many people with mania also exhibit wild behaviors such as constant partying and sexual promiscuity that lead to the breakup of marriages and other relationships. Holly describes how her bipolar ex-husband suddenly left his family: "The heartbreak occurred when, during a manic high, he decided to divorce me and marry another woman, leaving the kids and me to make it on our own."[19]

Frequent hospitalizations also put a burden on family members and often mean that the patient cannot contribute financially or personally to relationships. It is not unusual for patients to spend 25 percent of their time in a hospital, according to the National Institute of Mental Health (NIMH). And during this time they end up losing about fifteen years of productivity. This has many repercussions in all aspects of a person's existence.

Some other typical behaviors of patients with bipolar disorder are equally to blame for the failure of relationships and for ongoing disruptions in everyday life. Many patients abuse drugs and alcohol, which can exacerbate symptoms and lead to violent behavior. Violent behavior most frequently occurs during a manic or mixed state episode in which the individual is agitated and irritable. The experience can be extremely traumatic and even dangerous for family members.

Many patients with manic-depressive illness also have anxiety disorders that make them extremely difficult to live with. These anxiety disorders include post-traumatic stress disorder and obsessive-compulsive disorder. Post-traumatic stress disorder keeps an individual in a shell-shocked state as though the person just experienced a very traumatic event. The person is unstable and prone to emotional outbursts. Obsessive-compulsive disorder involves repetitive behaviors such as constantly cleaning the house. The person experiences anxiety if the behavior is not carried out.

People with bipolar disorder also have a higher than normal risk of death, and this can place a strain on relationships as well as introducing an element of instability. One extremely challenging risk is suicide. Approximately 25 percent of people with the disease attempt suicide and about 10 percent of patients succeed. Just living with the threat of suicide is unsettling for both the patient and family members. As novelist Danielle Steele revealed in testimony to the United States Congress after her son with bipolar disorder committed suicide at age nineteen:

> By 15, I believed he was suicidal. He never put it in words, but was so often depressed and so isolated that I was afraid to go into his room, sure that I would find him dead, by his own hand. I know now that my instincts were right. When I read his journal after his death, I discovered that from the age 11 on, he had written about killing himself every single day. It took another eight years to accomplish it.[20]

Accidental deaths are also more frequent among people with bipolar disorder, particularly in the manic phase, in which delusions of in-

During manic episodes, people with bipolar disorder can suffer from delusions of invincibility and engage in high-risk behaviors such as jumping from a cliff.

vincibility and immense power may lead individuals to do risky things such as drive too fast or jump off a cliff. Death from cardiovascular, endocrine, respiratory, or infectious diseases is also more likely to occur in patients with bipolar disorder. This may be because many patients smoke cigarettes, which increases the risk of these diseases. It also may be partly due to the fact that many patients engage in reckless sexual behavior, which places them at risk for infectious and sexually transmitted diseases such as AIDS. Experts say that people with mental illness are also less likely to seek medical attention for these types of medical problems, thereby putting them at even greater risk of death. Either way, the increased risks and time spent ill can be especially difficult on patients.

Special Problems with Bipolar Children

Mental health authorities say that the relationship and lifestyle problems associated with bipolar disorder can be especially challenging when the patient is a child. With children, episodes tend to be rapid cycling and particularly intense. This poses problems for parents and other caretakers and in school. Sometimes hospitalization is the only alternative. Jerry, for example, would lie, steal, set fires, destroy property, and hurt himself. His mother, Cheryl, could no longer cope, so she put him in the hospital.

Placing Jerry in the hospital at age nine was the hardest thing I have ever had to do. But it was also the best choice I could have made. It took the treatment team three weeks to diagnose him and find the correct medication combination that worked for him. The child who came home to me was smiling and loving, and he started remembering the things he had enjoyed like Nintendo, bike riding, and roller-blading.[21]

Many other parents do not find such a positive outcome with treatment and must deal with a child's challenging behavior on a daily basis. Sigrid describes what life is like in a household with a very unstable child with manic-depressive illness, Rose:

Crucial coping strategies at our house and in the families I've met include a sense of humor, a tolerance for eccentricity, flexibility, and support from other parents. We call our angelic-looking little girl with the blonde hair and big brown eyes "Mountain Goat" for her facility at scaling the kitchen cupboards, and send her to a summer camp that offers climbing lessons where she can safely indulge her need for risk-taking. We have accepted that we must be prepared to leave any sit-

The disruptive behavior and roller-coaster mood swings of children with bipolar disorder can sorely test parents and teachers.

uation that Rose finds overwhelming, and [as an example of eccentricity] don't mind cooking artichokes for breakfast at times. In a parent support group, we discover that all of our kids have, at one time or another, attempted to jump out of a moving car; we are not surprised to find that they share a deep affinity with animals, and an innate spirituality. Our kids often blame us for their rages, emotional hijackings in which their hair-trigger limbic systems perceive even the gentlest parental guidance as nuclear attack and react accordingly . . . many days I wonder how I'll survive the roller-coaster mood swings, the creativity utilized in devising yet another scheme to test my patience (the latest photocopying our Siamese cat), and an intensity that can exhaust several adults in a day. It is heartbreaking to witness one's young child trash her room in a rage, then threaten to kill herself, sobbing "why do I have to cry all the time?"[22]

Besides the problems that they may create at home, children with bipolar disorder can be disruptive at school and often must receive special education. Most children with the disease qualify as disabled, and the Individuals with Disabilities Education Act passed by the United States Congress in 1975 requires that public schools provide an Individualized Education Program (IEP) for each child who is disabled. Once a child is in an IEP or other special education program, he or she may suffer from the stigma of being different or mentally ill. This can bring on other problems that remain with the child, such as social isolation, but in general a special education program is necessary.

Methods of Coping

Whether patients with bipolar disorder are children or adults, experts say there are many things that can be done to ease the burden of day-to-day life. One is maintaining hope that the disease can be managed and having a positive attitude about the future. Ginny, a patient with bipolar disorder, says that the key to maintaining a positive attitude is realizing that the bad times do not last and will change. Another thing she has found helpful is joining a support group, where she can both receive and give encouragement to other people like her. Support groups share information about the disease and offer personal insight into treatment options and coping techniques. They often have speakers and social events and help patients and families become advocates for themselves and others. Some support groups meet over the Internet, while others meet in person. Many are sponsored by nonprofit groups, while others meet informally.

Other patients say that maintaining a positive attitude involves setting and keeping realistic and achievable goals. For someone who is having a severe depressive episode, realistic and achievable goals may be very small and seemingly minor things such as getting out of bed, bathing, and eating a good meal. That may be all that a seriously depressed person can realistically achieve in a day. For someone who is manic, a realistic goal might be to try to stay focused on one activity instead of jumping from one activity to the next. Such goal setting can help to positively channel energy and control the episodes of mood swings. These goals can center around chores, health, sleep, nutrition, work, relationships, hobbies, learning, and many other areas.

In addition to maintaining a positive attitude, patients with bipolar disorder can take several measures to make their lives as stable as possible. These include being responsible for taking medications regularly and keeping appointments with the psychiatrist or psychotherapist. Getting educated about the disease is also important, as this allows a patient to make informed decisions about treatment and lifestyle issues. Also important is developing a plan for monitoring symptoms and for dealing with events so as not to allow mood swings to get out of control. This includes following a daily routine of a healthy diet, exercise, and plenty of sleep to give as much stability as possible. The person is also advised to look for signs of irritability, reckless behavior, or suicidal tendencies and to take appropriate action, such as calling the doctor or entering the hospital. Talking to close family members or friends in advance and developing a plan of action for when an episode of mania or depression is coming is also a good idea. For example, some patients instruct their loved ones to take away their credit cards in the event

Joining a support group can help families and friends cope with the difficulties of living with a loved one suffering from bipolar disorder.

that they begin an episode of mania or to lock up firearms and pills to prevent suicide in case of depression.

Things Families Can Do

Experts also recommend things that families can do to make their lives and the life of the patient easier. One is attending a support group or counseling to help sort out and work through the plethora of emotions they are feeling about the patient and the illness. Many people experience emotions ranging from guilt to shame, and it is important to talk with others who understand. This is especially vital for parents of children with bipolar disorder, because they bear the responsibility for administering medication and otherwise caring for the child in addition to coping with the everyday stresses brought on by the disease.

Another thing family members can do is to educate themselves about the disease so as to have realistic expectations. This helps

Depression and Bipolar Support Alliance Support Group

The Depression and Bipolar Support Alliance (DBSA) is one of the primary national nonprofit organizations that provide education and support to bipolar patients. It sponsors a network of local support groups designed to help patients and their families cope with everyday life. The DBSA says on their Web site what support groups can offer:

As independent affiliates of DBSA in their communities, DBSA chapters offer more than 1,000 peer-run support groups where you will find comfort and direction in a confidential and supportive setting, and where you can make a difference in the lives of others. The selection of services offered differs by chapter, depending on the needs of its members. Most groups are volunteer run and provide self-help through facilitated meetings. They are not group therapy; however, our chapters have professional advisors—a psychiatrist, psychologist, nurse or social worker from the community.

In addition to participating in the group sessions, you will meet people from your community who can relate to your experiences and you may learn valuable information about mental health professionals and services in your area as well as tips and techniques others use to manage their illness.

Some chapters offer services in addition to their support groups, such as educational sessions, newsletters, lending libraries and special events. Some offer information on mental health professionals in your area or upcoming mental health legislation in your state.

family members understand that the patient has a real disease that he or she cannot snap out of at will. Family members will comprehend that the patient is not merely weak or flawed, and this will hopefully make it easier to offer unconditional love, support, and patience. Educated family members also can help the patient by recognizing when the person needs immediate medical help, such as when he or she discusses suicide or starts to become manic. They also can emphasize to the patient the importance of regularly taking medications and can be supportive of positive efforts the patient makes.

Dealing with Stigma

While patients and families have to deal with the reality of everyday life with bipolar disorder, they also must confront the stigma associated with a mental illness. Many affected people say that this stigma is one of the most difficult aspects of living with a disease such as bipolar disorder.

This stigma can present itself in many ways. Many people with bipolar disorder lose friends and spouses because others are uncomfortable with their mental illness. Jennie, for example, a teen with bipolar disorder, found that many of her former friends wanted nothing to do with her after her symptoms began. Victoria, a woman with bipolar disorder, found that people at her church looked at her strangely and avoided her once they found out she was mentally ill. Others with bipolar disorder find that the illness affects their ability to obtain or keep a job because of their employers' attitude. Once an employer knows that an employee has manic-depressive illness, they may be reluctant to continue to keep the individual. The federal Americans with Disabilities Act protects people from any discrimination in employment because of a disabling disease. While it is illegal to fire someone because he or she has an illness, an employer can fire someone for failing to perform the job adequately during acute episodes of mania or depression or for taking excessive time off work to deal with these episodes.

However stigma and discrimination present themselves, many patients develop methods to help diminish these problems. Some

Stigma and Mental Illness Throughout History

Stigma attached to mental illness has been a major problem throughout history. From the Stone Age through the Middle Ages, people viewed mentally ill individuals as being possessed by demons. Several methods of dealing with the mentally ill included drilling holes in the skull to release the demons, burning the person at the stake, and boiling the person in water.

During the seventeenth and eighteenth centuries, mentally ill people were treated as prisoners. They were put in filthy cells, where they were often chained to the walls, whipped, and put on public display like animals in a zoo. In the eighteenth and nineteenth centuries, several doctors and other reformers, such as Dorothea Dix in the United States, began advocating the humane treatment of the mentally ill. Some mental hospitals began treating these individuals kindly, but there were still many abuses and much scorn and mistrust of mental illness. It was not until the 1950s and 1960s that advocacy groups began to lobby for better treatment and decreased the stigma of the mentally ill. But then the introduction of new medications to treat severe mental illnesses such as bipolar disorder led to a great many people with mental illness being released from mental hospitals to live in communities. Unfortunately, many patients stopped taking their medication and were not being treated at all. Many of these people became homeless or committed crimes, which did not help the image of the mentally ill among the public.

To this day, some people believe that persons with mental illness are weak-willed individuals who should be shunned. These people are embarrassed to associate with anyone with a mental illness. Advocacy groups today are more active and successful in changing public perceptions of mental illness, especially as scientists present more evidence that illnesses such as bipolar disorder are brain diseases. But there is still a long way to go before the stigma of mental illness is a thing of the past.

use humor, as Victoria, who developed bipolar disorder as a teen, explains: "One of the ways I cope with it is [by] using a sense of humor. I've been known to say, 'Oops! That was a bipolar moment.' It seems to put people at ease."[23]

Anne, who grew up with bipolar disorder, has become a vocal advocate for people with bipolar disorder as part of her efforts to deal with stigma. She encourages others to "complain. Yell. Scream.

Dorothea Dix, a Civil War nurse, was an outspoken advocate for the humane treatment of the mentally ill.

Report stigma in the media. Complain to insurance companies. We need fairness and respect. . . . I am like you, or your friend, or your lover, or your child. I have bipolar disorder, manic depression. And my voice WILL be heard."[24]

There are also several well-known people with bipolar disorder who publicly advocate better perceptions and treatment of people with the disease. They have done a great deal to improve the public's view of bipolar disorder and mental illness in general. These advocates include former Boston Red Sox baseball player Jim Piersall, author of the book *Fear Strikes Out*; actress Patty Duke, who wrote *A Brilliant Madness*; and writer/psychologist Kay Jamison, author of *An Unquiet Mind*. These and other advocates have brought the topic of manic-depressive illness into the open and have dispelled a lot of the mystery that used to surround the disease. They and others have brought new hope to the many patients who suffer daily with the effects of the disease and with the stigma associated with mental illness.

Diminishing the stigma and being given an opportunity to lead a productive life are indeed what most patients with bipolar disorder wish for themselves. As Toni, who has lived most of her life with manic-depressive illness, points out:

> My dream in life is very simple: to be a contributor to life rather than to take away from it. To all my brothers and sisters that suffer I want each of you to know that you don't suffer alone and you don't have to sit there and take it. There is treatment, there is hope, and there is a new horizon. It is just a little harder for those of us with this illness to reach our destination in life, but our battles can be victorious and our goals can be reached.[25]

Chapter 5

The Future

Although existing treatments can help many patients with bipolar disorder, some are not helped by existing drugs. Those with rapid-cycling bipolar disorder in particular are difficult to treat. In other cases, medications can work well for many years and then lose their effectiveness. Many patients also suffer from unpleasant side effects from medications. All these factors mean that new and better treatments are necessary. There is also a need for greater understanding of the causes and diagnosis of the disease, and toward this end, research in several areas is ongoing in the hopes of providing a brighter future for those who live with manic-depressive illness.

Research into Diagnosis

Some researchers are focusing on improving diagnostic techniques for bipolar disorder so it is not misdiagnosed. Several studies are looking at how diagnostic criteria for bipolar depression and the related unipolar depression agree or disagree. Unipolar depression is a disease that involves depression but no mania. Researchers are hoping this will aid clinicians in making a correct diagnosis. Studies also are looking at whether unipolar mania is a distinct disease, suggesting that perhaps new categories of diagnosis are needed to cover different forms of the disease in different people.

Another area in which researchers are striving to improve diagnosis is among children and adolescents. Diagnosis is often difficult in these age groups, because many times the symptoms resemble ADHD or similar illnesses. Some studies are currently focusing on methods of distinguishing these disorders and of determining whether one or more of them is present at the same time in a particular individual.

Research into Causes

There is a great deal of research being conducted into the various causes of bipolar disorder. One area of investigation involves questions about why the disorder sometimes begins late in life. Generally, manic-depressive illness starts between early and mid-life, but sometimes it begins later. Researchers are studying why this happens and have discovered several things. One is that adults with late-onset bipolar disorder report less family history of the disease and more blood vessel disease that occurs along with the bipolar disorder. This suggests that other physical illnesses may play a large role in triggering late-onset bipolar disorder and that genetics may play a significant role in early onset cases of the disease.

In order to ensure proper diagnosis of bipolar disorder and to improve treatment options, mental health researchers are studying the possible causes of the disorder.

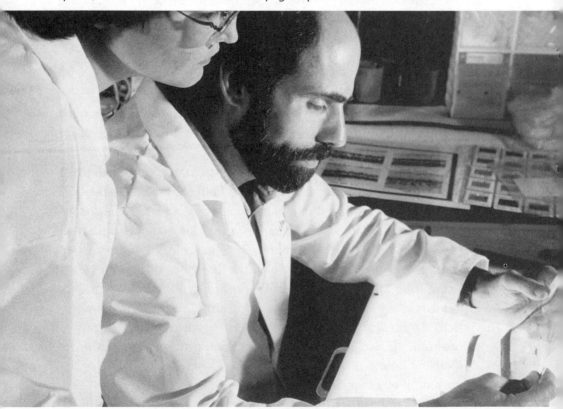

Another area of investigation is the causes for the greater incidence of rapid cycling among women compared to men. Three times as many women as men experience rapid cycling. One reason for this may be that women tend to take antidepressant medication more frequently than men do. Some antidepressants can induce mania, and investigators are studying whether this might be causing rapid cycling in women. Another factor being studied in this regard is thyroid hormone. Low thyroid levels have been associated with rapid cycling, and researchers have discovered that women with bipolar disorder are more likely than men with the disease to have a thyroid disorder. The thyroid disorder may be caused by lithium in many cases, but no one knows why lithium is more likely to cause a thyroid disorder in women than in men. Investigators are now studying whether the higher incidence of thyroid disorders and rapid cycling in women are related.

Several researchers are examining the role of different enviromental factors in causing bipolar disorder. One study is looking at how life events, stress, thought patterns, and personality affect the likelihood that people with cyclothymia, a condition characterized by periods of mild hypomania alternating with mild depression, will develop full-blown bipolar disorder. Cyclothymia is known to be a strong risk factor for bipolar disorder. But doctors do not know what factors determine whether or not a person with cyclothymia will go on to develop the more severe bipolar disorder. Research into these factors can lead to an understanding of how to possibly prevent the onset of manic-depressive disease.

Other factors that have been associated with the development of bipolar disorder are physical and sexual abuse in childhood. Because experimental results on these factors have been mixed, researchers are trying to find out what role they play in the subsequent development and course of the illness. One recent study evaluated a variety of patients, some of whom had experienced physical and sexual abuse as children and some of whom had not. The study found that those with a history of physical and sexual abuse tended to get bipolar disorder earlier, had increased incidence of drug and alcohol abuse, were more likely to have rapid cycling, had a higher rate of suicide attempts, and had more psychological stressors occurring before each manic or depressive episode. This indicates that not only can physical and sexual abuse play a role in causing bipolar disorder, but these factors may also contribute to making the disease worse in people who experienced these traumas during childhood.

Although most researchers have not found any correlation between diet and the onset of bipolar disorder, several doctors have suggested that a higher intake of seafood is associated with a lower probability of getting the disease. This is presumably due to the large amounts of omega-3 fatty acids that have been linked to a protective effect on the brain, although researchers are not sure how or why. A recent study found that people who ate more seafood were less likely to get bipolar disorder. This suggests that taking omega-3 fatty acids might be useful in preventing or treating the disease, and indeed, several researchers are now studying the value of giving bipolar patients this food supplement to see if it helps their condition.

Genetics, another known cause of bipolar disorder, is the subject of a great deal of research. One avenue of research involves studying the DNA of people with bipolar disorder and of families where two or more members have the disease to try to figure out which genes make people susceptible to the disorder. One gene that appears to influence the development of bipolar disorder is called G protein receptor kinase 3. This gene plays a role in regulating various neurotransmitters in the brain. Scientists believe that when this gene is mutated, the brain's response to the neurotransmitter dopamine in particular may be affected, leading to symptoms of bipolar disorder. Other genes that have been linked to the disease are the somatostatin receptor 5 gene, which influences dopamine metabolism, and myo-inositol monophosphatase, which seems to influence the brain's response to lithium.

Other researchers are studying abnormalities in brain chemicals that underlie bipolar disorder. One study is using PET scans to compare how well the neurotransmitter serotonin binds to receptors in bipolar patients and in healthy people. Previous studies have found that the function of serotonin is abnormal in people with bipolar disorder. The present study is measuring serotonin receptor activ-

Much of the research on the causes of bipolar disorder focuses on genetics. Geneticists like these believe that human DNA will provide an answer.

ity in several areas of the brain that appear to play a role in bipolar disorder. The researchers are measuring receptor activity both before and after the administration of mood-stabilizing drugs. Hopefully this research will offer some insight into the causes of bipolar disorder as well as into the mechanism of action of mood-stabilizing drugs.

Structural brain changes that may underlie bipolar disorder are another area of intense research. Several years ago, one study found that the brains of many people with bipolar disorder have so-called hyperintensities in the white matter of the brain. These are abnormal bright spots that appear on an MRI scan. Now scientists are attempting to learn more about these hyperintensities and their significance. One recent study, for example, found that these bright spots are often present in the brains of both adolescents and adults with bipolar disorder. But they do not appear in the brains of all people with manic-depressive illness, so their role in causing the disease is still in question. An alternate explanation is that the disease causes the hyperintensities rather than vice versa, but that too remains to be seen.

Another structural finding being investigated concerns the hippocampus, an area of the brain important in regulating emotions and motivation. Previous studies have found that the hippocampus is smaller than normal in many bipolar patients. A more recent study looked at the size of the hippocampus in identical twins, one with bipolar disorder and one without, and found that the structure was consistently smaller in the twin with bipolar disorder. This indicates that the size of the hippocampus may play a role in causing the disease, and further research is planned to find out more about this phenomenon.

Increased size of the ventricles, or canals, in the brain has been previously noted in bipolar patients. However, no one is sure if this structural brain change causes or results from the disease. A recent study sheds light on this question. Researchers used MRI to measure the volume of the ventricles in bipolar patients who had had many manic and depressive episodes, in patients who were experiencing their first bipolar episode, and in healthy subjects. The lateral ventricles were considerably larger in the patients with multiple bipolar episodes than in the first-episode patients or in the healthy people. Scientists think this indicates that there is a good probability that the enlarged ventricles are caused by bipolar episodes rather than that they cause bipolar disorder.

Research into Treatment

In addition to research into its causes, a primary area of research into bipolar disorder concerns treatment. A major project is being conducted at the NIMH to study the effectiveness of treatments for a variety of patients, including those in mental hospitals and those who live on their own. The researchers are following several thousand patients to assess the short- and long-term effectiveness of various treatment regimens and are attempting to formulate advice on possible treatments for patients who do not respond to therapy. They are also scientifically evaluating the effectiveness of combining medications and psychotherapy and are developing methods of implementing research findings into clinical practice.

This research, known as the Systematic Treatment Enhancement Program for Bipolar Disorder, will run for five to eight years at twenty test sites across the United States. Patients and their study doctors select a standard plan of treatment, and the doctor follows the patient's progress to determine its short- and long-term effectiveness.

Research at the National Institute of Mental Health

The National Institute of Mental Health (NIMH) is one of the primary centers and sources of funding for research into bipolar disorder. The NIMH is a component of the National Institutes of Health (NIH), the federal government's primary agency for medical and behavioral research. The NIH is part of the U.S. Department of Health and Human Services.

The NIMH conducts and sponsors research on all aspects of mental disorders. Some research is done in-house as part of the intramural research program. There are about five hundred scientists who work in this program in laboratories and with patients at the NIH Clinical Center. Other NIMH efforts are centered on the extramural program, which provides more than two thousand research grants at universities and other research institutions throughout the United States and overseas.

Whether the research is performed through the intramural or extramural program, the NIMH supports research into the causes, diagnosis, occurrence, and treatment of mental illness. The organization also communicates new information to scientists, the public, the news media, and mental health professionals in order to keep all these parties up-to-date on the newest research findings. The NIMH also supports the ongoing training of more than one thousand scientists to carry out basic and clinical research on all aspects of mental health.

Other researchers at the NIMH are studying the benefits of various types of psychotherapy in managing bipolar disorder. Their research is comparing the effectiveness of psychoeducation, cognitive behavioral therapy, family therapy, and interpersonal and social rhythm therapy. Effectiveness is measured in terms of how much the therapy motivates the patient to regularly take prescribed medications, how frequently the patient suffers acute manic or depressive episodes, and how quickly and effectively the patient gets back on his or her feet after an acute episode. Researchers are hoping to develop measures that indicate which type of psychotherapy will benefit which patient.

One additional avenue of research into factors that affect recovery from bipolar disorder focuses on social support. Social support is the ongoing psychological backing that a person believes he or she receives from significant others such as friends and family. Based on two questionnaires that measure perceived social support, researchers in one study discovered that those patients who perceived their social support system to be adequate tended to recover more fully and to not relapse as frequently as those who felt their social support level was lower. This indicates that forms of therapy that encourage strong interpersonal relationships and support can be especially valuable in a patient's recovery and in lessening the probability of relapse.

Some research is focusing not on psychotherapy treatment, but on ECT and related new techniques. One NIMH study is evaluating the effectiveness of ECT administered with antidepressant medication. This combination has not been scientifically assessed before. Other researchers are investigating newer brain stimulation techniques. One such technique is known as transcranial magnetic stimulation (TMS); a closely related technique is called repetitive transcranial magnetic stimulation (rTMS). Unlike ECT, TMS and rTMS do not produce brain seizures. With these procedures, a magnetic coil is placed against the scalp and a small electrical current flows directly into the parts of the brain directly beneath the coil. Researchers are targeting areas of the brain that show abnormal activity in bipolar patients, such as the dorsolateral prefrontal cortex. The electrical current causes neurons in the selected area to

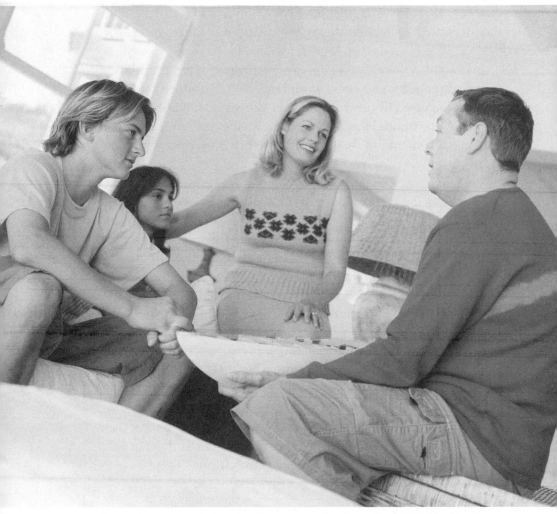

Researchers are exploring the therapeutic value for patients with bipolar disorder of social support networks such as friends and family.

fire, and for unknown reasons this helps to alleviate symptoms. In these experiments, TMS or rTMS are applied for twenty minutes daily for five to ten days. Preliminary results show that these treatments have been effective in alleviating symptoms in some patients for whom medication does not work. Side effects of TMS and rTMS may include headache and muscular soreness, but these do not appear to be serious and are of less concern than the side effects of ECT. Investigators have high hopes that these methods will prove to be effective alternative treatments for bipolar disorder.

In related research, scientists are testing another stimulation technique called vagal nerve stimulation (VNS), which was originally developed to control epilepsy. Doctors who administered the procedure noticed that the treatments helped improve the mood of epilepsy patients, so they decided to test it on people with bipolar disorder who did not respond to medication.

VNS involves the use of a device similar to a pacemaker. A doctor implants the device under the skin on the left side of the collarbone and connects an electrode to the vagus nerve in the neck. The VNS device is programmed to stimulate the vagus nerve for thirty seconds every five minutes while it is on. The stimulation alters the production of the neurotransmitters norepinephrine, serotonin, GABA, and glutamate in the brain. So far investigators have found that the VNS treatments improve mood disorders in about one-third of the patients tested. They plan to do further research to try to improve the technique for use as a possible routine treatment for bipolar disorder that does not respond to other treatments. However, according to one of the doctors involved in VNS research, because the procedure involves permanently implanting a device, "you would never use it unless people had exhausted most of their other options — that is, failed several medications and either ECT or, if available, transcranial magnetic stimulation (TMS)."[26]

Research into Drugs

Some of the research into treatment is focusing on existing and new drugs. Research on existing drugs is primarily designed to determine exactly how these drugs work. Studies on lithium, for example, are looking into how this widely used drug functions as a mood stabilizer. Some scientists are focusing on an enzyme called protein kinase C because they now know that lithium reduces this enzyme in the brain. These researchers are looking at both whether protein kinase C plays a role in causing bipolar disorder and exactly how lithium's effect on this enzyme alleviates symptoms. Other scientists are looking at other chemicals that

TMS and rTMS

Transcranial magnetic stimulation (TMS) and repetitive tran-scranial magnetic stimulation (rTMS) are among the most promising new techniques for the treatment of bipolar disorder. The first TMS device was built at the University of Sheffield in England by Anthony Barker in 1985. It was designed as a tool for diagnosing neurological diseases. But soon researchers realized that it could be used to map regions of the brain involved in memory, sensation, muscle control, and emotions, particularly once an improved magnetic core enabled scientists to deliver more and faster pulses known as rTMS to specific areas of the brain.

Researchers also realized that the technique had the potential to treat certain mental and neurological diseases because of its ability to excite neurons in a particular area. They began testing it as a treatment for depression in the early 1990s, and since then it has been found to effectively treat this disorder by changing activity in the dorsolateral prefrontal cortex region of the brain. Research on whether or not rTMS helps bipolar disorder is much newer. It appears that bipolar patients respond differently to rTMS than do patients with unipolar depression; in fact, in some studies the treatments produced mania in formerly depressed patients who were bipolar. Obviously, more research must be done before TMS or rTMS can be approved for treating manic-depressive illness.

lithium seems to affect, such as phosphatidylinositol-4,5 bis-phosphate. The role of this chemical in bipolar disorder has not yet been proven.

Other research into existing drugs is looking at their effects on children, who typically respond to these drugs differently than adults do. In order to be formally approved for use in children,

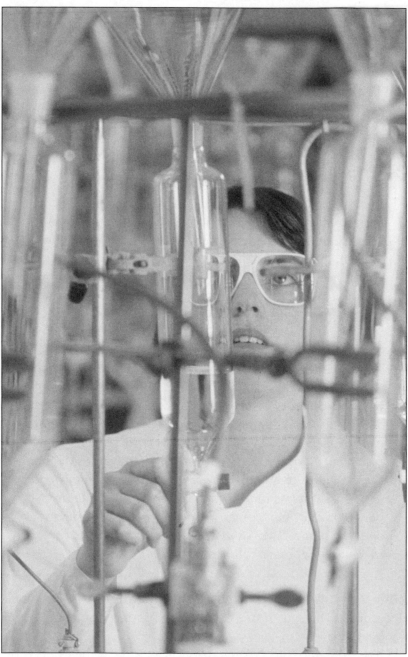

A researcher tests a drug compound in a laboratory. Research laboratories are currently developing a host of new drugs to treat bipolar disorder.

these drugs must be tested on children. This means that the children's parents must give special permission for these youngsters to be part of a study involving the drugs in question. One study, for example, is looking at how effective valproate is for the treatment of acute manic episodes in children and adolescents. Another study is testing the safety and effectiveness of various antidepressants for patients in these age groups.

As for new drugs being tested, there are presently many under investigation as possible treatments for bipolar disorder. New drugs are invented in a laboratory and tested on laboratory animals. Once a compound has been proven to be safe and effective in a laboratory setting, the drug's developer may apply to the FDA in the United States or to comparable agencies in other countries to begin testing on humans in clinical trials. Clinical trials are generally sponsored by a research institution or by a pharmaceutical company. They are set up at numerous hospitals and clinics throughout the nation. Patients can find out about and enroll in clinical trials through their physicians or through sponsoring agencies. All participation is voluntary with the understanding that the experimental drug may or may not help.

Clinical trials involve three or four phases of testing. Once these phases are completed in a satisfactory manner, the FDA may approve the drug for marketing, and doctors can begin prescribing it for people not included in the clinical trials. Drugs previously approved to treat one disease and being tested to treat another condition also must go through clinical trials to be approved for treatment of the new condition.

Drugs Being Tested

One drug being tested is a completely new type of treatment for bipolar disorder. The drug is called mifepristone, and it blocks receptors for glucocorticoids, a type of steroid that exists naturally in the body. Researchers believe that glucocorticoids may play a role in certain mood disorders, and they are hoping that by blocking these chemicals mifepristone will have antidepressant effects.

Another drug being studied in clinical trials is riluzole. This drug is currently approved to treat Lou Gehrig's disease, a severe degenerative disease of the central nervous system. Researchers are now testing riluzole to treat acute depression in patients with bipolar disorder who take a mood stabilizer. Preliminary results showed that the drug produces antidepressant effects in some patients who are not helped by other antidepressants. Investigators are hoping that riluzole will provide a new alternative for the treatment of depression in bipolar patients.

Several researchers are investigating existing drugs for use as mood stabilizers. The anticonvulsants lamotrigine and gabapentin, for example, are currently used to treat epilepsy and are being evaluated as possible mood-stabilizing treatments in patients with bipolar disorder who are not helped by existing mood stabilizers.

The drug tamoxifen, currently used to treat breast cancer, is also being tested as a mood stabilizer. Researchers at the NIMH believe that tamoxifen may be effective in this regard because it inhibits the chemical protein kinase C in the brain. Investigators have previously found that the mood stabilizers lithium and valproate both inhibit protein kinase C, but no one has yet proven that this is how these drugs work to control bipolar disorder. The researchers who are testing tamoxifen believe that because it is a strong protein kinase C inhibitor, these tests will help determine whether other mood-stabilizing medications work by interfering with this chemical. This would go a long way toward understanding the underlying causes of bipolar disorder. Plus, tamoxifen could prove to be an effective alternative mood stabilizer that would offer patients who are not helped by other mood stabilizers a new opportunity for treatment.

Hope for the Future

The object of all of this research, whether it involves new drugs, genetics, or brain chemicals, is to better understand bipolar disorder and to formulate new and more effective treatments. According to Lana R. Castle in her book *Bipolar Disorder Demystified*, this research should give hope to patients looking for relief from a disease that presents constant challenges and disruptions. She says that one improvement is the rise of holistic treatments, which address both the mind and body: "Having a mood disorder is no

New psychotropic medications that researchers are developing are only part of more effective treatment programs for bipolar disorder.

Bipolar disorder can interfere with life both on and off the job. Research into treatment offers hope for all afflicted with the illness.

reason to give up hope. Pharmaceutical companies are constantly developing more effective psychotropic medications with fewer side effects. And as scientists and doctors learn more about the brain and mind-body connection, treatments are becoming more holistic."[27]

Although researchers have a long way to go toward understanding bipolar disorder, mental health authorities believe that patients and their families have good reason to believe that current and future research will lead to better lives for those who suffer from the disease.

Notes

Introduction: An Increasingly Common Disorder

1. Quoted in E. Fuller Torrey and Michael B. Knable, *Surviving Manic Depression*. New York: Basic Books, 2002, p. 11.

2. Torrey and Knable, *Surviving Manic Depression*, p. 15.

Chapter 1: What Is Bipolar Disorder?

3. Quoted in Lana R. Castle, *Bipolar Disorder Demystified*. New York: Marlowe & Co., 2003, p.15.

4. Quoted in Torrey and Knable, *Surviving Manic Depression*, p. 31.

5. Quoted in National Institute of Mental Health, "A Story of Bipolar Disorder (manic depressive illness)," www.nimh.nih. gov/publicat/bipolstory02.cfm.

6. National Institute of Mental Health, "Child and Adolescent Bipolar Disorder: An Update from the National Institute of Mental Health," www.nimh.nih.gov/publicat/bipolarupdate. cfm.

Chapter 2: What Causes Bipolar Disorder?

7. National Institute of Mental Health, "Bipolar Disorder," www.nimh.nih.gov/publicat/bipolar.cfm.

8. Torrey and Knable, *Surviving Manic Depression*, p. 129.

Chapter 3: How Is Bipolar Disorder Treated?

9. National Institute of Mental Health, "Bipolar Disorder," http://www.nimh.nih.gov/publicat/bipolar.cfm.

10. Torrey and Knable, *Surviving Manic Depression*, p. 248.

11. Torrey and Knable, *Surviving Manic Depression*, p. 137.

12. Castle, *Bipolar Disorder Demystified*, p. 210.

13. Quoted in Remedy Find, "Psychotherapy: Cognitive Behavioral Therapy (CBT)," www.remedyfind.com/rm-2852-Cognitive. asp.

14. Quoted in UPMC News Bureau, "Interpersonal and Social Rhythm Therapy May Offer Patients with Bipolar Disorder an Improved Chance of Long-Term Health," http://news bureau.upmc.com/WPIC/BipolarIpsrt.htm.

Chapter 4: Living with Bipolar Disorder

15. Castle, *Bipolar Disorder Demystified*, p. 3.

16. Depression and Bipolar Support Alliance, "Ginny—Coping Skills That Work," www.dbsalliance.org/stories/Ginny.html.

17. Depression and Bipolar Support Alliance, "Becky—Young and Recovering," www.dbsalliance.org/stories/Becky.html.

18. Depression and Bipolar Support Alliance, "Angel—There Is Help and Hope," www.dbsalliance.org/stories/Angel.html.

19. Depression and Bipolar Support Alliance, "Holly—My Ex-Husband's Illness," www.dbsalliance.org/stories/Holly.html.

20. YourCongress.com, "Danielle Steele, Bipolar Disorder, and Suicide," www.yourcongress.com/ViewArticle.asp?article_id =79.

21. Child and Adolescent Bipolar Foundation, "Jerry's Story: Early Onset Bipolar—a Mother's Perspective," www.bpkids.org/learning/reference/articles/002.htm.

22. Child and Adolescent Bipolar Foundation, "Parenting a Bipolar Child—a Mother's Thoughts," www.bpkids.org/learning/reference/articles/009.htm.

23. Depression and Bipolar Support Alliance, "Victoria—No Longer in Fear and Isolation," www.dbsalliance.org/stories/Victoria.html.

24. Depression and Bipolar Support Alliance, "Anne—Who I Am," www.dbsalliance.org/stories/Anne.html.

25. Depression and Bipolar Support Alliance, "Toni—Fighting the Illness," www.dbsalliance.org/stories/Toni.html.

Chapter 5: The Future

26. Quoted in Neuropsychiatry Reviews, "VNS: An Epilepsy Treatment Shows Promise For Depression,"www.Neuropsychiatryreviews. com/feb00/npr_feb00_VNS.html.

27. Castle, *Bipolar Disorder Demystified*, p. 351.

Glossary

bipolar disorder: A disorder in which an individual's mood shifts from extreme highs to extreme lows.

chromosome: The wormlike body in the center of a cell where genes reside.

cyclothymia: A condition similar to bipolar disorder but characterized by much milder episodes of mania and depression.

depression: An illness in which the individual feels sad and hopeless.

gene: The part of a DNA molecule that transmits hereditary information.

hypomania: Mild to moderate mania.

mania: The phase of manic depression in which a person has a lot of energy and overly positive feelings.

manic-depressive illness: Bipolar disorder.

neurotransmitter: A brain chemical involved in sending messages between nerve cells.

rapid cycling: A form of bipolar disorder in which a person has four or more manic-depressive episodes within one year.

schizoaffective disorder: A disease similar to bipolar disorder that produces ongoing symptoms of schizophrenia.

Organizations to Contact

Child & Adolescent Bipolar Foundation
1187 Wilmette Ave., PMB #331
Wilmette, IL 60091
(847) 256-8525
www.bpkids.org

This organization offers information and support on all issues related to bipolar disorder in children and adolescents.

Depression and Bipolar Support Alliance (DBSA)
730 N. Franklin St., Suite 501
Chicago, IL 60610-7204
(312) 642-0049
(800) 826-3632
fax: (312) 642-7243
www.dbsalliance.org

This organization offers information and support on all aspects of bipolar disorder.

National Alliance for the Mentally Ill (NAMI)
Colonial Place Three
2107 Wilson Blvd., 3rd Fl.
Arlington, VA 22201-3042
(703) 524-7600
(800) 950-6264
fax: (703) 524-9094
www.nami.org

The National Alliance for the Mentally Ill offers information, advocacy, and support on all aspects of mental illness.

National Institute of Mental Health (NIMH)
Office of Communications
6001 Executive Blvd., Room 8184, MSC 9663
Bethesda, MD 20892-9663
(301) 443-4513
(866) 615-6464
fax: (301) 443-4279
wvw.nimh.nih.gov

This federal government agency provides information on all aspects of bipolar disorder, including causes, treatment, research, and living with the disease.

National Mental Health Association (NMHA)
2001 N. Beauregard St., 12th Fl.
Alexandria, VA 22314-2971
(703) 684-7722
(800) 969-6642
www.nmha.org

The National Mental Health Association offers education, advocacy, and research to benefit those who have mental illnesses.

For Further Reading

Helen A. Demetriades, *Bipolar Disorder, Depression, and Other Mood Disorders*, Berkeley Heights, NJ: Enslow, 2002. Written for teens, this book discusses the disease, treatment, research, and case studies.

Judith Peacock, *Bipolar Disorder*, Santa Rosa, CA: Lifematters, 2000. This book describes bipolar disorder and special problems faced by teens.

Michael Sommers, *Everything You Need to Know About Bipolar Disorder and Manic Depressive Illness*, New York: Rosen, 2000. This is a comprehensive book on bipolar disorder written for teens.

Works Consulted

Books

Samuel Barondes, *Mood Genes*. New York: W.H. Freeman, 1998. Describes the search for genes that may be responsible for mental disorders.

Lana R. Castle, *Bipolar Disorder Demystified*. New York: Marlowe, 2003. Easy-to-understand book on all aspects of bipolar disorder based on the author's personal experience with the disease.

E. Fuller Torrey and Michael B. Knable, *Surviving Manic Depression*. New York: Basic Books, 2002. Comprehensive book about all aspects of bipolar disorder.

Periodicals

Kim M. Cecil et al., "Proton Magnetic Resonance Spectroscopy of the Frontal Lobe and Cerebellar Vermis in Children with a Mood Disorder and a Familial Risk for Bipolar Disorders," *Journal of Child and Adolescent Psychopharmacology*, vol 13, no. 4, 2003.

Depression and Bipolar Support Alliance, "Helping a Friend or Family Member with a Mood Disorder."

Mani N. Pavuluri et al, "Recognition and Treatment of Pediatric Bipolar Disorder," *Contemporary Psychiatry*, April 2002.

Internet Sources

Child and Adolescent Bipolar Foundation, "Five-Year-Old Boy Responds to Two Mood Stabilizers." www.bpkids.org/learning/reference/articles/010.htm.

———, "Jerry's Story: Early Onset Bipolar—Mother's Perspective." www.bpkids.org/learning/reference/articles/ 002.htm.

———, "Parenting a Bipolar Child—a Mother's Thoughts." www.bpkids.org/learning/reference/articles/009.htm.

Depression and Bipolar Support Alliance, "Alison—Learning to Live with Myself." www.dbsalliance.org/stories/Alison.html.

————, "Angel—There Is Help and Hope." www.dbsalliance. org/stories/Angel.html.

————, "Anne—Who I Am." www.dbsalliance.org/stories/Anne. html.

————, "Becky—Young and Recovering." www.dbsalliance. org/stories/Becky.html.

————, "Bipolar Disorder." www.dbsalliance.org/info/bipolar. html.

————, "Blair—I Have Survived." www.dbsalliance.org/stories/ Blair.html.

————, "Chuck—Open All Night?" www.dbsalliance.org/stories. Chuck.html.

————, "Facts About Bipolar Disorder." www.dbsalliance.org/ Media/BipolarFacts.html.

————, "Ginny—Coping Skills That Work." www.dbsalliance. org/stories/ Ginny.html.

————, "Holly—My Ex-Husband's Illness." www.dbsalliance. org/stories/Holly.html.

————, "Toni—Fighting the Illness." www.dbsalliance.org/stories/ Toni.html.

————, "Victoria—No Longer in Fear and Isolation." www. dbsalliance.org/stories/Victoria.html.

National Institute of Mental Health, "Bipolar Disorder." www. nimh.nih.gov/publicat/bipolar. cfm.

————, "Child and Adolescent Bipolar Disorder: An Update from the National Institute of Mental Health." www.nimh.nih. gov/publicat/bipolarupdate.cfm.

————, "A Story of Bipolar Disorder (Manic Depressive Illness)." www.nimh.nih.gov/publicat/bipolstory01.cfm.

Neuropsychiatry Reviews, "VNS: An Epilepsy Treatment Shows Promise for Depression." www.neuropsychiatryreviews.com/ feb00/npr_feb00_VNS.html.

Remedy Find, "Psychotherapy: Cognitive Behavioral Therapy (CBT)." www.remedyfind. com/rm-2852-Cognitive.asp.

UPMC News Bureau, "Interpersonal and Social Rhythm Therapy May Offer Patients with Bipolar Disorder an Improved Chance of Long-Term Health." http://newsbureau.upmc.com/WPIC/bipolarIpsrt.htm.

YourCongress.com, "Danielle Steele, Bipolar Disorder, and Suicide." www.yourcongress.com/ViewArticle.asp?article_id=79.

Index

Picture Credits

Cover photo: © Images.com/CORBIS
© Andrew Brookes/CORBIS, 31
© CORBIS, 75
Jeff Di Matteo, 35
© Historical Picture Archive/CORBIS, 9
L. Innamorati/Photo Researchers, Inc., 63
© Michael Keller/CORBIS, 91
© LWA-Stephen Welstead/CORBIS, 25
John Madere/CORBIS, 15
Will and Deni McIntyre/Photo Researchers, Inc., 60, 71, 78, 88
© Bill Miles/CORBIS, 46
NASA/Kennedy Space Center, 28
© Richard T. Nowitz/CORBIS, 81
© Gabe Palmer/CORBIS, 11, 27
PHANIE/Photo Researchers, Inc., 52
PhotoDisc, 41, 68
Photos.com, 17, 38, 43, 48, 55 (background), 58, 64, 67, 85, 92
© Tom Stewart/CORBIS, 56
Voisin/Photo Researchers, Inc., 26
Steve Zmina, 14, 21, 22

About the Author

Melissa Abramovitz grew up in San Diego, California, and developed an interest in medical topics as a teenager. She began college with the intention of becoming a doctor, but she later switched majors and graduated summa cum laude from the University of California, San Diego, with a degree in psychology in 1986. She launched her career as a writer in 1986 to allow her to be an at-home mom when her two children were small, realized she had found her niche, and continues to freelance regularly for a variety of magazines and educational book publishers. In her eighteen years as a freelance writer, she has published hundreds of nonfiction articles and numerous short stories, poems, and books for children, teenagers, and adults. Many of her works are on medical topics. At the present time she lives in San Luis Obispo, California, with her husband and two college-age sons.